PUBLIC SPEAKING

50 Lessons on Presenting Without Losing Your Cool

Joe Serio, Ph.D.

To Roger –
Best wishes.
Joe
1/cy

Project Manager: Jennifer Bailey
Design Team: Harriet Brewster and Jena Rodriguez

For information, contact GTN Media at info@gtnmedia.com

Printed in the United States of America
ISBN 13: 978-0-9900216-0-5

www.joeserio.com

Contents

PART 2
PREPARATION:
THE KEY TO PUBLIC SPEAKING SUCCESS

PART 3
THE PRESENTATION: GETTING THE NERVE

PART 4
INTO THE ARENA:
SETTING OUT ON YOUR JOURNEY   115

THE TAKEAWAYS   120

ACKNOWLEDGEMENTS   124

ALSO IN THE GET THE NERVE™ SERIES   126

BIOGRAPHY   129

The long span of the bridge of your life is supported by countless cables called habits, attitudes, and desires. What you do in life depends upon what you are and what you want. What you get from life depends upon how much you want it, how much you are willing to work and plan and cooperate and use your resources. The long span of the bridge of your life is supported by countless cables that you are spinning now, and that is why today is such an important day. Make the cables strong!

~ L.G. Elliott

About the *Get the Nerve*™ *Series*

The idea for the *Get the Nerve*™ *Series* grew out of my personal transformation from being fearful of most things to facing that fear and achieving more than I thought possible.

My goal is to share what I have learned so that you, too, can see the possibility for your own life and make it a reality.

Each book in the series begins with reflections on fear. This builds the foundation for the following lessons, which are specific to the topic of each book. As L.G. Elliott says in the quotation on the facing page, "Your life is supported by countless cables called habits, attitudes, and desires." This series is a blueprint for helping you create and strengthen the cables of your bridge, so you can live the most inspired life you can imagine.

I would love to hear about changes you make in your life as a result of the *Get the Nerve*™ *Series*. Please contact me with your stories of personal transformation at drjoe@joeserio.com.

Other Titles in the *Get the Nerve*™ *Series*

Overcoming Fear: 50 Lessons on Being Bold and Living the Dream

Time Management: 50 Lessons on Finding Time for What's Important

Effective Communication: 50 Lessons on How to Hear and Be Heard

Leadership: 50 Lessons on Inspiring Others to Be Their Best

Emotional Intelligence: 50 Lessons on Knowing Who You're Dealing With

Introduction

*For, usually and fitly, the presence of an introduction
is held to imply that there is something of
consequence and importance to be introduced.*

~ Arthur Machen

I was that person. You know the one I mean – nauseated stomach, sweaty hands, dry mouth. The very idea of public speaking would send me into a panic.

In elementary school, I couldn't read aloud in class without shaking. In high school, I couldn't attempt to recite poetry without suffering a brain freeze. In college, I walked to class short of breath, afraid I'd be called on by the professor. My knees knocked together so loudly while giving a presentation, I was certain my classmates could hear it. Any kind of public speaking petrified me.

Fear and anxiety took control. My brain got so scrambled I couldn't think straight. Crash and burn.

That's the bad news.

The good news? All of that has changed.

Through practice, mistakes, self-observation, and study, I learned the secrets of effective public speaking. This sweaty, nauseated, bundle of nerves now gets up – willingly, gladly – in front of any audience.

I've spoken before 1,000 people for three hours and had a blast. And more importantly, the audience enjoyed it and benefited from it.

Public Speaking: 50 Lessons on Presenting Without Losing your Cool is a nuts and bolts prescription – a road map – that anyone can use in any public speaking situation. Master the lessons in this book, and you will change your life.

Part 1

Managing Fear: It's a Mind Game

A Fate Worse Than Death?

*It is not the critic who counts; not the man
who points out how the strong man stumbles, or
where the doer of deeds could have done them
better. The credit belongs to the man who is actually
in the arena, whose face is marred by dust and
sweat and blood; who strives valiantly; who errs,
who comes short again and again, because there is
no effort without error and shortcoming; but
who does actually strive to do the deeds; who knows
great enthusiasms, the great devotions; who spends
himself in a worthy cause; who at the best knows
in the end the triumph of high achievement, and
who at the worst, if he fails, at least fails while
daring greatly, so that his place shall never be with
those cold and timid souls who neither know
victory nor defeat.*
~ Theodore Roosevelt

It has been said that people fear public speaking more than death, prompting comedian Jerry Seinfeld to quip, "Which means if you are like the majority of people, at a funeral you would rather be in the casket than giving the eulogy."

True or not, it is a fact that the mere thought of public speaking can intimidate the hardiest of souls. But it doesn't have to be that way.

Fear of public speaking is generated by psychologically-created obstacles. What if I make a mistake? What if I embarrass myself? What if I'm criticized?

There are two critical things to remember:

First, you will make a mistake, you will feel embarrassed, and you will be judged. So what? Once you accept this – and realize there are ways to plan for, minimize, and recover from mistakes gracefully and successfully – the sky's the limit.

Second, we often compare our insides to other people's outsides. We envy their outward appearances of confidence and focus on our own inner fears. It's important to realize that they have fears just as we do.

The key is having a road map to navigate those fears.

- If we allow ourselves to put aside the blinding fear for a second, we can see that acquiring skills – including effective public speaking – has an internal logic, some basic rules and processes to follow.

- These rules and processes are the road map to success, available to anyone who seeks it.

- With public speaking, many audience members believe they could not be at the front of the room and therefore never try. To paraphrase Henry Ford: If you think you can, you're right. If you think you can't, you're right.

- There are countless successful public speakers. They aren't necessarily any smarter or more talented than you. They put their fear in perspective and start on their journey.

- The road map shows them how to manage their fear each and every time they speak, whether it's while giving a speech, teaching a class, or making a toast.

- They know very well that 95% of becoming an excellent public speaker is a mental game. They know that it depends on self-motivation. They know that mistakes are not fatal.

If they can do it, WHY NOT YOU?

TAKEAWAY: A good road map will help you manage your fear.

Lesson 2
The Power of Belief

Luke: I can't believe it.
Yoda: That is why you fail.

~ "Star Wars"

As you work to overcome your self-created
limitations, talk to your subconscious,
telling it that instead of reacting, you're now going
to respond with conscious choices.

~ Wayne Dyer

It's critical to understand that, ultimately, our biggest obstacles are our self-limiting beliefs.

This may be the single most important idea to grapple with as we imagine the kind of life we want. It's frequently the only thing standing between us and success.

The issue isn't really about knowing how to do something. Everything we need to know is out there just waiting for us to pick it up.

We know how to lose weight. We know how to become a millionaire. We know how to get good grades in school. We even know how to land on Mars. And, yes, we know how to become excellent public speakers.

The central issue is typically one of desire, focus, and discipline.

Here's a keystone question to ask yourself: "Have I decided what I want?" Don't take this word "decided" too lightly. We either decide or we don't decide; there is no in between.

Once you've decided that you truly want to be a public speaker, ask yourself: "Am I committed to it?" We're either truly committed or we're not. Don't fool yourself. We can't be committed to an undertaking and not committed at the same time.

Do you believe you can have what you want, and are you willing to do what it takes to get it? If so, then the only thing left to do is go get it.

Now think about your fear of public speaking. Can you face an audience? Yes. Can you talk? Yes. Can you read, write, and prepare your presentation? Yes. Can you relate some event from your life to illustrate a point for the audience? Yes. Can you learn to create a Microsoft® PowerPoint™ presentation if necessary? Yes.

So, what's stopping you?

Throughout our lives we're influenced by the needs, demands, and reactions of those around us. We spend so much time trying to understand what others want us to be that we forget to go after our dreams. Excuses, blame, and other manifestations of fear can become such ingrained habits to the point where we barely realize they are holding us back. We forget what's possible. But, like any habit, we can change this (Lesson 10).

This simple exercise of realizing that everything you need is already here is a critical step in managing your fear and moving forward.

Once you truly believe that your biggest obstacle is the way you look at yourself and your situation, your ability to do something about it will improve dramatically.

TAKEAWAY: Everything you need is already within you. It's time to believe in yourself.

Lesson 3

The Courage to Create

*The difference between try and triumph is
a little umph.*

~ Marvin Phillips

*Courage is not the absence of despair; it is, rather,
the capacity to move ahead in spite of despair.*

~ Rollo May

We frequently look at a finished product and enjoy it for what it gives us, forgetting – or perhaps never realizing – all the work involved.

And it doesn't matter what the product is. It could be a car, a movie, clothing, a ballet, a song, this book, whatever. And, yes, even a presentation.

When the product reaches an especially high level of craftsmanship, it's even easier to take it for granted. When it looks effortless, it looks easy. We sometimes even tell ourselves, "That's easy. I can do that."

But we can fail to appreciate the countless hours of planning, research, rehearsing, performing, building, and re-building – a lot of hard work – that went into making the final product look "easy."

It's frequently not until we try our own hand at it that we realize the mastery involved.

Think about performance artists like comedians, actors, musicians, painters, and many others.

Before we see comedians on an HBO special, for example, they have written, edited, performed, re-written, re-edited, and performed their material hundreds of times. They practiced countless times in private, in rehearsal, and on small stages long before they ever made it big.

The courage to create always begins with a single, small, first step. We decide what we want. We dedicate ourselves to the endeavor. We continue on the road, come what may.

Remember, once upon a time, Eric Clapton didn't know how to play guitar, Beyonce didn't know how to sing, and Gabriel "Fluffy" Iglesias didn't know how to tell a joke.

As the philosophers say, courage is the ability to act *in spite of* fear, not in its absence. That's why we talk about managing fear rather than overcoming fear.

One way to manage fear effectively is to appreciate the amount of work that goes into creating an excellent product. When we have no illusions about the hard work required for the task we set before us, we can get to work.

Embracing the process of working hard – preparation – is critical to reducing fear and getting the nerve to reach our goals.

As you work on your public speaking, remember that each presentation – regardless of the type – will require focused work with numerous adjustments being made along the way. That's all right. That's the way it's supposed to be.

TAKEAWAY: The key to your success is hard work focused on a specific objective.

Lesson 4

Managing Fear to Move Forward

The only thing we have to fear is fear itself.

~ Franklin Delano Roosevelt

*Love is what we were born with. Fear is what
we learned here.*

~ Marianne Williamson

As always, we have a choice. We can allow fear to prevent us from doing things we dream about, or we can find a way to manage our fear and move forward into things we never dreamed possible.

When we realize that everyone – even the most successful among us – has fear, we'll find it easier to move forward. When we realize that perfectionism – not to be confused with excellence – has no role in the creative process, we'll find it easier to move forward. When we realize that the universe is rooting for our success, we'll find it easier to move forward.

In our mind's eye, we can frequently look at the totality of what we're trying to accomplish and bury ourselves in fear. When we realize that creativity – and living – is about what we do here and now, in this minute, we'll find it easier to move forward.

Here are some useful ways to rethink fear and its role in your public speaking experiences:

*   Realize that our fear can be a result of interpretations of events from childhood, a time when we were not particularly qualified to accurately interpret what was happening around us.

- Resist the urge to compare how you feel on the inside to how others appear on the outside. It may seem that they're fearless. They're not.

- Understand the difference between healthy fear and paralyzing fear. Use fear as a motivator rather than as an inhibitor.

- Create mechanisms, games, and psychological tricks to counteract the fear that gets inside of you.

- Working hard beforehand will help reduce fear. Proper preparation prevents poor performance.

- Don't try to complicate or overthink your task. Just the opposite – KISS: Keep It Super Simple. The goal is to connect with, not confuse, the audience.

- Frequently visualize yourself giving a great presentation. Your mental rehearsal will create a habit that your body will follow.

- Learn breathing exercises to calm yourself before a presentation. (http://www.write-out-loud.com/overcoming-public-speaking-anxiety-breathing-exercises.html)

- Speak whenever possible. Experience is really the only way to learn public speaking, and mistakes are merely doorways to opportunity.

- Do your best to serve others. Public speaking is never about you. It's always about your audience. And the audience is there to learn, not judge you. Putting your ego to the side and serving others helps reduce fear.

TAKEAWAY: Managing fear can provide the key to unlocking all of your dreams.

Lesson 5

Planning the Journey

Plan your progress carefully; hour-by hour, day-by-day, month-by-month. Organized activity and maintained enthusiasm are the wellsprings of your power.

~ Paul J. Meyer

The best way to sound like you know what you're talking about is to know what you're talking about.

~ Unknown

Let's say we're going on a week-long trip by car. There are certain preparations we will need to make, a number of questions we will need to answer. Where do we want to go? What is the best route to get there? Should we have a mechanic look at the car before we go?

You get the idea. Ideally, we'll consider as many issues and requirements in advance as possible. The more questions we can answer, the less uncertainty and fear we're likely to experience.

Thinking through as many of these issues as possible while preparing your presentation is a great way to manage fear. The more you prepare, the fewer surprises you're likely to experience.

Preparation is one of the keys to reducing fear of public speaking (Lesson 16). Not only will your pre-performance anxiety decrease, you will look more confident as you deliver your presentation.

Questions to be considered include:

- What am I trying to accomplish?
- What message am I trying to convey?
- Who is my audience?
- How many people will be there?
- What is the speaking venue like?
- Will I need a microphone?
- Will I be standing or sitting?

The questions are numerous and most are applicable regardless of the type of speaking you're doing.

One of the most important aspects of your preparation from the outset is identifying the theme of your presentation, the main points you want to make, and the supporting information, experiences, and stories you will use to strengthen your argument and bring your theme to life.

Not to be overlooked is the fact that you should prepare with the assumption that things will go wrong. But if you have planned as thoroughly as possible, anticipating problems, you will already have with you knowledge, resources, and confidence. This makes it infinitely easier to focus on challenges when they do arise, without getting flustered (Lesson 45).

Creating a presentation is very much like any other journey: We need to decide where we're going and then create a map to help us get there.

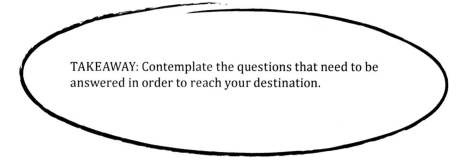

TAKEAWAY: Contemplate the questions that need to be answered in order to reach your destination.

Lesson 6

Become a Chinese Farmer

All that we are is the result of what we have thought.

~ Buddha

*Between stimulus and response there is a space.
In that space is our power to choose our response. In
our response lies our growth and our freedom.*

~ Viktor Frankl

In managing fear and maintaining perspective, I have found it very useful to keep in mind the story of the Chinese farmer that I read in *Buddhism: Plain and Simple* by Steve Hagen.

One day, the only horse of a Chinese farmer runs away. The farmer's neighbor runs over and exclaims, "How terrible! Your horse ran away." The farmer responds, "Who knows what's good or bad?"

The next day the horse returns with 50 other horses trailing. The neighbor runs over and exclaims, "How wonderful! You have 50 new horses." The farmer responds, "Who knows what's good or bad?"

While breaking in one of the new horses, the farmer's son is thrown and breaks his leg. The neighbor runs over and exclaims, "How terrible! Your son broke his leg." The farmer responds, "Who knows what's good or bad?"

The next day the Chinese military comes through the town conscripting all the young males but not the farmer's son because of his broken leg. The neighbor runs over and exclaims, "How wonderful! They didn't take your son." The farmer responds, "Who knows what's good or bad?"

Where does this story end? If we're the neighbor, it never does. If we're the farmer, it just is what it is.

If we're like the neighbor, we will be shifting with the wind every time it changes direction. We will find ourselves on an emotional rollercoaster, responding to the superficial nature of events.

The farmer understands the nature of the universe and the nature of the human condition.

Most of us create our own stress, our own insecurity, our own fear, through our interpretation of what happens around us.

Events are events. Once an event has occurred, we can't undo it. The only thing we have control over is our response to the event. It is our response that will determine which outcome we get. If we choose to respond in a negative, unhealthy way, we will get a negative, unhealthy outcome.

We can be our own worst critics and beat ourselves up for what we deem to be bad performances.

After one very dissatisfying presentation I gave, the program organizer, knowing I was down on myself, said, "How would you grade your presentation?" I responded, "F." He said, "If I had to give it a grade, I would say B minus" and explained why. He showed me that "good" and "bad" are issues of perception and judgment.

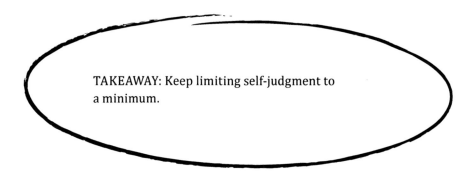

TAKEAWAY: Keep limiting self-judgment to a minimum.

Lesson 7

Learn to Love the Plateau

*If people knew how hard I worked to get my
mastery, it wouldn't seem so wonderful at all.*

~ Michelangelo

*In the realm of ideas everything
depends on enthusiasm; in the real world all rests
on perseverance.*

~ Johann Wolfgang von Goethe

When we try something new, our first steps are frequently filled with mixed emotions. We're excited about the prospect of a new beginning. Doors are opening that hadn't before.

We're stretching and growing and dreaming about possibility. We set out on a steep learning curve and seem to be absorbing so much very quickly. It's exciting and fun.

At the same time, we can feel anxious, uncertain, and filled with trepidation. After all, learning something new can be scary. It will force us to leave our comfort zone.

We're taking a chance putting ourselves out there because most of us have been conditioned to worry about failure. "What if I make a mistake?"

All of that is OK because nothing great ever happens without leaving our comfort zone and making mistakes.

After a while, though, it will seem that we're not making as much progress as we had been. The excitement and novelty of our new venture starts to wear off, and we hit a plateau.

While it may feel that we have stalled, this is actually a natural occurrence. We can't remain on a steady, upward path; there will be ebbs and flows in our progress.

The challenge is to recognize when we hit a plateau and understand what it really means.

The plateau – especially the first one – is where many of us become frustrated and simply quit.

With a mindset of frustration and impatience, it can be difficult to realize that another leap of progress is awaiting us up ahead.

The trick is to understand that plateaus happen, and fairly often. It's critical to keep going – without judgment, second-guessing, or quitting – and simply continue to work.

In public speaking, we may be criticized and judged over and over. I had very thin skin when I started public speaking and felt embarrassed regularly. Like I said at the beginning of this book, I couldn't do it in high school and college or for most of my twenties.

That was a very painful plateau to be on. It was only by continuing to work through my pain and get more experience that I could pass that plateau and jump to the next level.

TAKEAWAY: Remember, plateaus are a critical part of mastering your subject matter.

Lesson 8

Embracing Imperfection

Striving for excellence motivates you; striving for perfection is demoralizing.

~ Harriet Braiker

Ring the bells that still can ring
Forget your perfect offering.
There is a crack in everything.
That's how the light gets in.

~ Leonard Cohen

Before we learn to put fear in perspective, we frequently go along from day to day with the baggage of the past – misunderstood, unresolved, weighty, festering – and superimpose it onto our present lives.

Perfectionism is one of the ways our fear can show itself.

Perfectionism frequently arises from our need to get the attention and love of figures we look to for validation, like parents, siblings, friends, peers, colleagues, and teachers.

We come to think that it is through our accomplishments that we make ourselves worthy of love and respect.

Fortunately, your audience is neither expecting – nor does it really want – "perfection."

Of course, your comments, speech, or presentation has to be planned, practiced, and effectively delivered. But, first and foremost, your audience is looking for connection, not perfection.

We may not realize that the standard we set for ourselves – or that we may perceive someone else has for us – is based on an often undefined, intangible, and probably unattainable ideal. Often, we have little idea of what those authority figures really want or what we're really aiming for as we try to please them.

And, even if we did reach it, we're not likely to be told that we're now "perfect."

The following is a very important fact to keep in mind that will help you avoid getting stuck in the quicksand of fear: Perfection is unattainable.

And there's a very good reason for that. We view everything through the prism of our own attitudes, values, beliefs, and experiences. What may resonate with me may not resonate with you. Someone will disagree with your point of view. And that's natural.

Convincing ourselves we must be "perfect," we frequently develop the reflex of saying, "I can't do this. It won't be perfect. I won't be perfect." That reflex stems in part from our personal narrative, the story of our life's wounds and sensitivities that we're still carrying, our perceived failure to measure up, or our failure to gain approval.

In public speaking, it's not our purpose to get our audience to approve of us. Our job is to serve the audience. Audiences want to be entertained, informed, and persuaded. They want to hear a speaker who is sincere, genuine, and authentic. Perfection is not required to do that.

Decide and commit to crafting the best presentation you can, with the understanding that there will always be room for improvement.

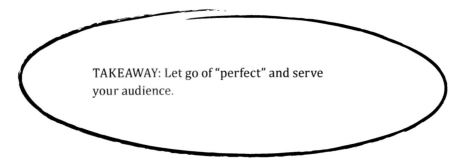

TAKEAWAY: Let go of "perfect" and serve your audience.

Just Do It

*The difference between who you are and who you
want to be is what you do.*

~ Bill Phillips

*Among the aimless you often hear talk about killing
time. People who are constantly killing time
are really killing their own chances in life. Those
who are destined to become successful are
those who make time and use it wisely.*

~ Arthur Brisbane

Procrastination is one of the methods we use in psychological warfare with ourselves when we're trapped in a battle with perfectionism. We can get caught in the push-pull of feeling we need to be perfect and yet realizing we need to make mistakes in order to learn.

Before you know it, procrastination is your habit; it's the way you live your life. And some of us have been doing it for so long that we don't even realize that our lives are passing by. We've convinced ourselves that we can't, and so we don't.

We get inside our own heads and repeat the mantras of childhood. "I have to please my parents." "I work better under pressure." "I don't know how to do it." "My worth is equal to my performance." "I want it to be perfect."

Try this simple exercise:

- Put aside one hour and start to scribble ideas and notes to use in a presentation. It could be an assignment for school, a briefing at work, a toast at a wedding, or simply a talk you've always wanted to give but have been afraid.

- Don't think about it, just get to work.

- Limit distractions. Turn off your cell phone. No interruptions.

- Set yourself up for success.

- After one hour, stop and take a look at what you were able to accomplish.

Remember, it doesn't have to be perfect; it just has to be sincere and authentic. Editing and shaping will come later.

Appreciating what you can accomplish in one hour will change how you look at time.

If you previously thought you couldn't make much use of fifteen or thirty minutes like I did, do the exercise again with that amount of time. Your mind will begin to shift to realize the possibilities.

Whereas before you may have sat in front of the television to kill that thirty minutes (which turned into two hours), now you see how using even such a seemingly small amount of time can work in your favor.

Bear in mind that overcoming procrastination doesn't happen overnight. It is often tied to complex issues (like perfectionism) that need to be worked on over months or years.

You are bound to find yourself on plateaus much of the time. Remember – that's OK. That's where you're supposed to be.

TAKEAWAY: Develop a plan today of the next steps you will take to manage your procrastination.

Lesson 10

Excuses and the Blame Game

How strange to use "You only live once" as an excuse to throw it away.

~ Bill Copeland

I attribute my success to this: I never gave or took an excuse.

~ Florence Nightingale

The two excuses I hear most often about public speaking are: But what if I embarrass myself? But what if I make a mistake?

Don't worry, you will feel embarrassed, and you will make a mistake. So what? Audiences won't remember, and you will have learned valuable lessons.

Why is it that some people can achieve everything they want and other people do nothing? They both have the same amount of time available to them. And they both have access to excuses. What makes them different?

The blame game can be a convenient and comfortable way to avoid fear and to spend our time criticizing others. By doing so, we don't have to face our own shortcomings and take responsibility for the position we're in.

Unfortunately, it also keeps us from moving forward, from accomplishing what we need to, and from being successful in life.

The blame game can take many forms. We typically use excuses as a way of fostering self-limiting beliefs while blaming everything and everyone but ourselves. Excuses are essentially a way for us to quit before we even start.

- But it will be difficult.
- But it will take a long time.
- But there will be family drama.
- But I don't deserve it.
- But no one will help me.
- But it has never been done.
- But I'm not strong enough.
- But I'm not smart enough.
- But I don't have time.
- But I don't have the money.
- But I don't have the energy.

The list goes on and on.

The thing that distinguishes those who rely on excuses from those who don't is attitude. We have the power to choose. We can choose to blame our childhood for our lack of progress. We can choose to blame our lack of resources. Or we can choose to be happy, adopt a positive attitude, and fight for the life we want. Successful people have courage; they're able to act in spite of their fears. And we can choose to be courageous.

Don't forget: If you think you can, you're right. If you think you can't, you're right.

TAKEAWAY: Get off your "buts" and take control of your own destiny.

Face the Brutal Facts

*Every time I've had a bad performance at an event,
I've come back more determined and focused.*

~ Shaun White

*A good athlete always mentally replays
a competition over and over, even in victory,
to see what might be done to improve the
performance the next time.*

~ Frank Shorter

It's easy to give in to fear and not act.

If we don't act, we can spare ourselves the anxiety of having to face a less-than-perfect self.

If we do act, and it doesn't go well, we're forced to acknowledge that we're not perfect and risk shame, guilt, and other uncomfortable emotions.

But once we choose to realize that perfection, procrastination, and blaming are no-win situations, we can move forward.

In his book, *Good to Great*, author Jim Collins discusses the attributes of great companies, one of which is the ability to face the brutal facts. Only by objectively assessing performance and being willing to make adjustments did these companies excel.

And, of course, this doesn't apply just to companies. One way to rein in fear and improve our public speaking is to muster up the courage to look at our shortcomings in the cold light of day.

Don't take this lightly. Performance assessment is critical to success. And, when you think about it, relentless review is a no-lose proposition.

You can congratulate yourself for what went well, and you can identify necessary changes for improvement. Over time, you will recognize your progress, and your audiences will appreciate your skill.

The more you step up to speak with a system of review in place, the less intimidating fear will become. And you just might shorten your time on the plateau before the next leap of progress.

Think about the rock group, U2. After every concert they meet with their manager to talk about what went well and what needs work.

The U.S. Navy precision flying team, the Blue Angels, does the same. After a performance, the pilots assemble to analyze the flight and to discuss what could be done better.

It's not a coincidence that U2 and the Blue Angels are considered among the best in the world in their fields.

Get the nerve to face the brutal facts about your speaking performance by recording it, passing out evaluation forms if appropriate, or getting feedback from people who heard you speak.

Commit to making steady improvement. You will be comfortable in front of a group before you know it.

TAKEAWAY: Paying close attention to critiques of your performance will get you further than blame and procrastination.

Lesson 12

Public Speaking as a Keystone Habit

Thoughts lead on to purposes; purposes go forth in action; actions form habits; habits decide character; and character fixes our destiny.

~ Tryon Edwards

I never could have done what I have done without the habits of punctuality, order, and diligence, without the determination to concentrate myself on one subject at a time.

~ Charles Dickens

When we think about public speaking strictly from the point of view of fear – as something that will bring us pain – it is easy to overlook the many significant advantages that getting comfortable with public speaking offers us.

Since many of us are stuck in the mode of looking at the negative side of public speaking, we can fall into the trap of thinking it's just about getting up in front of a group and risking our ego. But, actually, it's so much more than that.

For me, it's invaluable to remember that public speaking is a keystone habit – a single habit that positively impacts many areas of my life.

Let me give you an example of a keystone habit: losing weight. When you set out to lose weight, you impact many other parts of your life.

You change your eating habits, which means you're also paying more attention to how you spend your money.

You make time for working out, thereby improving your time management.

Your clothes fit better, you have more energy, and you're more confident.

So, just by losing weight, you can impact your health, money, time, self-esteem, and more. You get the idea.

It's the same pattern with public speaking. Once you put fear in perspective and start speaking, so many things in your life can change.

Public speaking will give you confidence, showing you that you can successfully manage your fears.

This success will transfer confidence to other challenges in your life.

For instance, you'll gain confidence in interacting with other people, which will influence your networking abilities and expand the circle of opportunities that become available to you.

It can impact your income; you may be given more responsibility at work or choose to use your new skill set and confidence to look for a better job.

Public speaking can positively affect your relationships at home and help you to empathize more with others' situations and needs since that is exactly what you will be doing with your audiences.

You will be bringing your insights to your audiences and will have a chance to inspire them to do more with their own lives. It doesn't get much better than that.

TAKEAWAY: Develop public speaking as a keystone habit that will change your life.

There's No Such Thing as Public Speaking

I try to bring the audience's own drama to them.

~ Judy Garland

The 7 Habits of Highly Effective People:
1. Be Proactive
2. Begin with the End in Mind
3. Put First Things First
4. Think Win-Win
5. Seek First to Understand, Then to be Understood
6. Synergize
7. Sharpen the Saw

~ Stephen Covey

In Lesson 1, we acknowledged that fear exists and that effective public speakers have learned to manage fear. They have a road map.

As we approach the point of preparing for our speaking journey, we might remind ourselves of Stephen Covey's advice from *7 Habits of Highly Effective People* – Begin with the End in Mind – and ask a basic question: What *is* public speaking?

You might think of public speaking as a situation in which you have to get up in front of an audience and deliver golden words with a silver tongue under hot spotlights.

The prospect of measuring up under such conditions could be overwhelming. You might think, "You want me to speak while all these people are looking at me?! What if I make a mistake? What if I feel embarrassed? What if they don't like me?"

If that's how you think about it, it's likely that you focus on yourself, your fear, and the physical and psychological challenge of speaking.

In other words, your ego may be dominating your thoughts. Suppress the ego, enlarge the heart.

Experienced and insightful public speakers don't think this way because they know two things you don't yet know:

1. You're just having a conversation (Lesson 14). In their book, *There's No Such Thing as Public Speaking*, Jeanette and Roy Henderson say that the goal of the "perfect" presentation is "to realize that the number of people listening is irrelevant; you are simply having a one-on-one conversation with a lot of people at once."

    For effective public speakers, a presentation is about sharing what they've learned from their experience, conversations, observations, and reading.

    It's about making a connection with the audience. It's about being sincere and authentic, just like any other worthwhile conversation.

2. It's *always* about the audience (Lesson 15). Thinking about public speaking as conversation means that the presentation is not about you, but about the audience.

    To Begin with the End in Mind means always focusing on giving the audience what it needs. This is your responsibility as a speaker.

    Once you can do that – and only if you can do that – the audience will give you what you need.

    The more you give, the more you will receive.

TAKEAWAY: Effective public speaking is a conversation focused on the needs of the audience, not your ego.

You're Having a Conversation

*Let us make a special effort to stop communicating
with each other, so we can have some conversation.*

~ Mark Twain

*The best speakers are the ones who do nothing more
than have a conversation with their audience.*

~ Richard Zeoli

Many of the elements of successful conversations feature prominently in public speaking. Below are eight key elements to keep in mind as you prepare your presentation. Most of these will be addressed in greater detail throughout the book. They're applicable in varying degrees depending on the type of public speaking you will be doing.

1. Find out a few things about the person you'll be talking to (if you can) before you actually start a conversation.

    It helps to know the issues facing a group before you make your presentation so that you can tailor your comments to their needs and make the strongest connection possible.

2. Ask questions so that the other person can talk about himself or herself.

    Whenever appropriate, give your audience members a chance to voice their opinions and share their experiences. This will enhance your connection.

3. Inject invitation and inspiration.

    Many public speaking occasions, whether a speech, presentation, wedding toast, or how-to session, can include stirring the audience to accept an invitation to act or to be inspired.

4. Listen actively.

    Listening is the most important communication skill. Learning how to use it effectively will help you hone in on the interests of the audience, guide the conversation, and express empathy when appropriate.

5. Forget yourself.

    Dale Carnegie once said, "It's much easier to become interested in others than it is to convince them to be interested in you." It's always about the audience.

6. Voice disagreement with respect.

    Your experience and opinion may be different from that of your audience. It's fine to disagree. Just be sure to maintain a professional demeanor at all times.

7. Accept occasional silences.

    Keep in mind that you don't have to fill every second of your presentation with talking. Audiences appreciate pauses and they can be very useful to you as the speaker (Lesson 43).

8. Know when the conversation has ended.

    As Winston Churchill noted, "Say what you have to say and when you come to a sentence with a grammatical ending, sit down."

TAKEAWAY: Put the needs of your audience first in the course of your conversation.

Lesson 15

It's Always About the Audience

Words have incredible power. They can
make people's hearts soar, or they can make
people's hearts sore.

~ Dr. Mardy Grothe

In public speaking, we must appeal either to the
prejudices of others or to the love of truth
and justice. If we think merely of displaying our own
ability, we shall ruin every cause we undertake.

~ William Hazlitt

I've said it before, and it bears repeating: Half the battle in managing fear of public speaking is remembering that a speech, presentation, or any other kind of public speaking is always about the audience.

Once you get comfortable with the idea of putting the audience's needs before your own, the energy that may have been paralyzing you with fear can be channeled into your efforts to create and deliver the best program possible.

So, what do audiences want?

- Audiences want you to succeed. Did you realize that? They are rooting for you! They know that if you do well, they will get what they came for.
- Audiences are typically understanding and forgiving as long as you're delivering what they need.

- Audiences want to be respected. They're spending their time, and sometimes their money, to listen to you.

- One key way to demonstrate respect is by showing up on time prepared to give your best and giving it.

- Words like "sincere," "genuine," and "authentic" are often used by audiences to describe effective public speakers.

- Audiences will overlook most mistakes if they sense you are well-intentioned.

- More than remembering what was said, audiences frequently remember how you made them feel. They will say things like, "That speaker was great! She was so funny!" or "What an incredible life he's had!"

- Even if it's a business presentation that requires facts and figures, your audience will remember if you were patronizing or boring.

- Respect, sincerity, and emotion are used to reach the pinnacle of a public speaking experience: making a connection with the audience.

- Audience members want to have a dynamic conversation with you.

- Stories, props, and humor can be effective tools in fostering a connection with an audience if appropriate for the setting and content. They have helped speakers reach audiences for centuries and, if used properly, can relax and engage even the most difficult audiences.

Public speaking is about performing a service for the audience. Knowing this helps reduce fear and nervousness and focuses your energy on creating the best possible presentation.

TAKEAWAY: Keeping the audience as your top priority helps reduce fear and improve performance.

Part 2

Preparation:
The Key to Public Speaking Success

Lesson 16
The Importance of Preparation

By failing to prepare you are preparing to fail.
~ Benjamin Franklin

There are no secrets to success. It is the result of preparation, hard work, and learning from failure.
~ Colin Powell

There is no way to overestimate the importance of preparation. Every aspect of your presentation depends on it.

Your audience will easily spot the difference between a speaker who is well-prepared and well-organized and one who didn't take the time to do it right. They will know if you violate the cardinal rule of public speaking: It's always about serving the needs of the audience.

Think of it this way: When you step before an audience, you're little different from the rock star going on stage, the comedian doing a TV special, or most any other performer. They have practiced for countless hours, writing, rewriting, and rehearsing.

The preparation is the hard work. The performance is the fun.

It will be fun for you and the audience, which means that a great performance doesn't come across as memorized.

In fact, if you prepare properly, you don't need to memorize your presentation at all.

Memorizing is fraught with danger – and anxiety. Forgetting your next line can create panic and make you stumble badly. You may come across as rigid and unnatural.

If you do need to follow a script, you just can't let it show. Well-prepared comedians, for example, know their material so well that even if there is a heckler in the audience, they can incorporate it into their act, get extra laughs, and smoothly return to their planned show.

If you'd prefer to work without a script, create triggers or reminders throughout your presentation that move you from one idea to the next.

A detailed outline helps organize the flow of your presentation. PowerPoint slides – especially with images – can be used as mile markers to push you into the next topic rather than act as a script that you read.

Know your material inside and out so you can navigate easily through it and recover from missteps gracefully.

Performers know how their presentation fits together.

Musicians don't stop playing if they hit a wrong note.

Actors don't leave the stage if they get a line wrong. They make up lines until they find their way back to the script.

Well-prepared speakers often do the same.

TAKEAWAY: Success or failure happens long before you get on stage. Thorough preparation can turn you into a winner every time.

Lesson 17

Know the Audience

*I see their souls, and I hold them in my hands, and
because I love them they weigh nothing.
[on audiences]*

~ Pearl Bailey

*An audience is never wrong. An individual member
of it may be an imbecile, but a thousand imbeciles
together in the dark – that is critical genius.*

~ Billy Wilder

Part of your job is to get to know the audience. You can do this in three ways:

1. If you are speaking at an event and there is a program organizer, ask that person about the makeup of the audience and the reason for the event. Is it a conference, a celebration, or a fundraiser? Is your presentation to be informational or persuasive? Ask the **program organizer how speakers** typically present to the audience. Do they use technology like PowerPoint or simply speak? Is there usually a question-and-answer session?

2. Conduct research about the audience beforehand. If it's a company, association, social or religious group, find out what issues it has been facing lately and customize your comments to the situation as appropriate. If you know the names of people you will be presenting to, particularly in a business setting, you can do research through social media, like LinkedIn®, to learn more about them. This tells the audience that you respect them enough to learn something about them and their industry.

3. Arrive early enough to speak with audience members before the presentation begins. When you can make a connection before the presentation, the audience is getting warmed up and may be responsive to you from the moment you begin your presentation.

Connect with the audience members, gauge their mood, break the ice, and make yourself accessible to them.

Once, I was speaking with executives about their legacy and the importance of setting an example.

I put WWJD on the screen and asked what it means. Everyone knew and said, "What Would Jesus Do?"

I brought up another that read WWJWD. One person knew and shouted out, "What Would John Wayne Do?" Everyone laughed.

The next slide read WWBGD. A woman slapped the arm of her colleague and jokingly said, "Hey, that's you. What Would Billy Goodman Do? Ha ha."

To their surprise, I said, "Yes, that's exactly right! Sometime down the road people who worked for you may say to themselves, 'What would Billy Goodman do in this situation?' And that will be part of your legacy."

No one in the audience knew I had gotten the conference roster from the organizer in advance. I succeeded in personalizing my message to the group, even in a seemingly small way. This played a role in my being the highest-rated among the twenty-two conference speakers my audience saw during the event.

TAKEAWAY: Knowing the audience is important in creating a connection and distinguishing yourself from other speakers.

Lesson 18

Build Your Triangle

*Oral delivery aims at persuasion and making the
listener believe they are converted.
Few persons are capable of being convinced; the
majority allow themselves to be persuaded.*

~ Johann Wolfgang von Goethe

*Then I asked: "Does a firm persuasion that a
thing is so, make it so?"
He replied: "All Poets believe that it does, and in
ages of imagination this firm persuasion removed
mountains; but many are not capable of a firm
persuasion of anything."*

~ William Blake

A critical part of your preparation will be to keep firmly in the center of your mind Aristotle's Rhetorical Triangle.

It's been around for more than 2,000 years, and you can't go wrong if you make it the foundation of your preparation.

We've already established that your presentation is *always* about the audience. While you're preparing your presentation, you have to make sure you're meeting the needs of the audience.

This is one of the three points of your triangle (Pathos).

Keep in mind questions like: Are my examples and imagery rich enough in detail to engage the audience's emotions and imagination? Am I appealing to the values and beliefs of the audience by using stories, characters, and information that audience members can relate to or care about? Am I trying to manipulate my audience or am I being authentic in my conversation with it?

The second point on the triangle is about you, the speaker (Ethos).

The presentation is always about serving the audience. The main questions are: Am I qualified to be addressing this particular audience on this particular topic? How have I connected myself to the topic of my presentation? Am I using the appropriate tone or voice to be effective in my delivery?

The third point on the triangle concerns the content being presented (Logos).

Being authentic (Ethos) and approaching the audience in the right spirit (Pathos) is all well and good, but if you fail to deliver the message in a structured, logical, and clear manner, Ethos and Pathos won't matter. You will not be able to persuade, inform, or entertain the audience. As you prepare your presentations, always bear in mind the following questions: Is my message clear and specific? Is my message supported by strong reasons and credible evidence? Is the argument logical and arranged in a well-reasoned order?

You must deliver all three points of the triangle. Weakness in any one of the sides of the triangle will cause the entire structure to collapse, i.e., your presentation will not be a success.

Excellent logic (Logos) and credentials (Ethos) will not save a speaker that fails to connect with the audience (Pathos).

Excellent logic (Logos) and a connection with the audience (Pathos) will not save a speaker that fails to persuade listeners that he or she deserves to be addressing the group (Ethos).

TAKEAWAY: Serve your audience by delivering a well-structured, logical presentation in an authentic way.

Lesson 19

Developing Your Presentation

*It usually takes more than three weeks to prepare a
good impromptu speech.*

~ Mark Twain

*Your purpose is to make your audience see what
you saw, hear what you heard, feel what you felt.
Relevant detail, couched in concrete, colorful
language, is the best way to recreate the incident as
it happened and to picture it for the audience.*

~ Dale Carnegie

You've done some research about the audience, but the fact is you may be uncertain about how to develop your presentation.

That's understandable. Here are some ideas.

Regardless of the topic, the essence of developing a presentation is collecting, processing, and organizing information.

Collecting information can involve numerous types of sources including the Internet, magazines, books, television, movies, songs, anecdotes, quotes, experiences, observations, imagination, and others.

Some people use scraps of paper, napkins, and envelopes to capture their ideas. Alternatively, you can use one of any number of apps to collect information. Here are three I like:

1. The notes app on your smartphone
2. Microsoft OneNote™ on your computer
3. Cloud-based backup, like Evernote® or Dropbox®, you can access from anywhere

Collecting means actively securing the information so that it's available at the moment you want to use it. Whether you prefer the low-tech or high-tech method, it's critical to have a specific container (notebook, box, folder, computer file, etc.) to collect all of your material. You never want to lose an idea.

Processing is primarily spending time with the material, thinking about it, turning it around in your mind, starting to look for angles, parallels, approaches – ways that you might consider organizing the information.

Don't overlook this step. This is where you put your personal stamp on the material. It will define you and your presentation for the audience.

Organizing the information primarily involves fleshing out the general shape of the presentation. For example, how will the arc of the presentation look – that is, what's the beginning, middle, and end?

Organizing can include drafting a quick outline to see what information you have, where there might be gaps, and if the initial flow makes sense.

You should also start thinking about any images, videos, photos, charts, and graphs that might help tell your story.

This is all very loose at this point. While the presentation may be taking on some kind of shape, you know that you'll make a lot of changes before the presentation is ready.

TAKEAWAY: Put a system of collecting, processing, and organizing information in place for ease in developing your presentation.

Shaping Your Presentation

*The wise ones fashioned speech with their thought,
sifting it as grain is sifted through a sieve.*

~ Buddha

*Creativity is just connecting things. When you ask
creative people how they did something, they feel
a little guilty because they didn't really do it, they
just saw something. It seemed obvious to them after
a while. That's because they were able to connect
experiences they've had and synthesize new things.*

~ Steve Jobs

By this time, you have been collecting information, thinking about the topic, and starting to organize your material. You have a very broad outline in place.

Now it's time to give the presentation a more definite shape.

For me, shaping the presentation has a lot to do with identifying the major points I want to make and how I'm going to make them.

- What is the underlying theme or lesson of the presentation? What message do I want to leave with my audience?

- What are the two, three, or four major points I want to make to support that theme? (The length of time allotted will influence the number of points I will be able to make.)

- What stories, anecdotes, experiences, or observations can I use to support the major points?

- What are my unique attributes? Would it be appropriate to use any of them in this particular presentation?

You will be tempted to cram as much information into your allotted time as possible. Resist this urge at all costs!

Make your major points, support them with illustrations, do a great closing, and sit down.

At a conference once, I watched a speaker who was short of time increase his tempo so much that he lost the audience.

Consider whether any of your talents can be infused into the presentation in an appropriate way. I've seen speakers paint, play the drums, do backflips and more. I frequently use a guitar or harmonica to illustrate points I'm making, if appropriate. Use personal touches to influence the shape of your presentation, but be absolutely sure they're appropriate.

In terms of the mechanics of shaping the presentation, I like to make as much progress as possible at this stage, so I tend to do this:

- Work for very focused periods of time with little interruption
- Try to utilize my high-energy period of the day whenever possible, which is typically from 6:00 - 10:00 am
- Select as many images, graphics, and other visuals as possible in one work session
- Consciously minimize the number of bullets and amount of text being used if it's a PowerPoint presentation

The shape of your presentation will emerge as you re-work, re-work, and re-work your material. Do not skip this step. Re-working is the difference between success and failure.

TAKEAWAY: Determine your theme and major points, personalize your presentation when possible, and re-work your draft.

Lesson 21

The Flow of Your Presentation

All the real work is done in the rehearsal period.

~ Donald Pleasence

*Action and reaction, ebb and flow, trial and error,
change – this is the rhythm of living. Out of our
over-confidence, fear; out of our fear, clearer vision,
fresh hope. And out of hope, progress.*

~ Bruce Barton

The flow of your presentation will determine how it's received by your audience. The classic structure of the overall flow of a presentation is to tell the audience what you're going to tell them, tell them, and then tell them what you told them. This will be an important guide for your arc – the beginning, middle, and end of your presentation.

- Begin your presentation with a compelling opening. Your task is to capture the audience's attention from the very first sentence you deliver. They want to understand quickly the point of the presentation and What's In It For Me (WIIFM). You can win them over or lose them in the first few minutes.

- Once the audience understands their benefit in taking the journey, you begin to unfold for them the theme and major points that you developed during your preparation.

- Energy and enthusiasm are indispensable in getting the audience on board and keeping their attention. Your flow will depend in large part on your animation, your commitment to the subject, and your ability captivate the audience.

- Aside from issues of logical flow, which you will consider when you're developing and shaping your presentation, the flow of the presentation *as you are delivering it* will be dependent on the speed and tone of your voice. If you need to convey excitement, make sure your voice conveys it. If you are coming to a dramatic revelation or conclusion, adjust your pacing as the situation requires, either slower for mounting anticipation or quickly for a sense of action.

- The flow will also be affected by your body language. For many presentations, audiences want to see a speaker who is calm, confident, and prepared. If the occasion calls for it, they want to see someone who is animated, smiling, and engaged. Your gestures and facial expressions must be in sync with your voice and the content of your presentation. Standing still and speaking in a monotone voice will be devastating to your flow.

- Be sure to vary the learning tools at your disposal as needed, particularly if it is a lengthy presentation. Visual learners will need to see your points written, auditory learners will need to hear it, and kinesthetic learners will need you to demonstrate it.

- Close strongly with a poignant story and a call to action, if appropriate (Lesson 47). Everything you have told your audience has led you to this moment. For example, inspire them to be better tomorrow if it's a motivational presentation. You could inspire them to learn more if it's a classroom setting. You might inspire them to improve productivity if it's a business setting.

Test the flow of your presentation by rehearsing it several times, in front of a mirror, in front of an audience of one, or in front of a group. If you have to rehearse it alone, be sure to always speak it out loud rather than "speaking" in your mind or reading it to yourself.

TAKEAWAY: Be conscious of the flow of your presentation. Start out strong, follow your established arc, and close by inspiring your audience.

Lesson 22

Beware of PowerPoint

*If your words or images are not on point, making
them dance in color won't make them relevant.*

~ Edward Tufte

*PowerPoint could be the most powerful tool on your
computer. But it's not. Countless innovations fail
because their champions use PowerPoint the way
Microsoft wants them to, instead of the right way.*

~ Seth Godin

Like any tool, PowerPoint can be a great way to enhance your work if you use it correctly.

But countless presentations have died a slow and boring death because many presenters simply don't use PowerPoint effectively.

Far too many speakers cram as many words as possible onto a single slide and read it. If your primary goal is to make a connection with the audience, asking them to read along is not going to cut it.

There are several problems with this approach.

- Turning your back on the audience for a length of time is disrespectful. You're losing them.

- If you're not using a microphone, they can't hear you when you turn around to read. You're losing them.

- A lot of words mean the audience is reading and not listening. You're losing them.

- If the audience is reading, they'll tire easily and be bored by your presentation. You're losing them.

As trainer Ken Brown notes, "PowerPoint is not a crutch, a lesson plan, or a substitute for knowing the material you're presenting. It's not going to make you a great presenter."

So what is it for?

To help you visually tell your story. Use as many photos, images, diagrams, videos, and other audio-visual support as reasonable to help tell your story. They're more memorable than words on a screen. They entertain the audience. And you won't lose the audience's attention because they're reading.

Ask yourself: "What will I do if there is a power failure or equipment failure?"

If you were planning on reading from your slides, you're dead in the water. But you will still have to give the presentation. The show doesn't end because something goes wrong.

You, not your slides, are responsible for telling your story.

Your presentation should be attractive but not unduly flashy:
- Graphics flying in, fading out, twirling, spinning, and bouncing distract the audience and take away from your message.
- Depending on your type of presentation, strive to have fewer than five bullet points on a slide.
- Don't write full sentences or paragraphs for bullet points.
- Be aware that poor color combinations and background designs can wash out or swallow text.

TAKEAWAY: Public speaking is about the audience, not the PowerPoint presentation. The fewer the words, the more powerful your message. Think about not using PowerPoint at all!

Lesson 23
Handout Material for the Audience

As a general rule, the most successful person in life is the one who has the best information.

~ Benjamin Disraeli

I was brought up to believe that the only thing worth doing was to add to the sum of accurate information in the world.

~ Margaret Mead

Handout material can be very useful for audiences.

Even in short presentations, especially keynote addresses, speeches, or other relatively brief public speaking situations, a one-page handout can help. In long sessions of several hours or even a day or two training or workshop, handout notes are necessary. Remember, it will depend on the goal of your presentation and the kind of journey you're on with your audience.

Along with props and other tools, handouts help to keep the audience's attention. That may seem counterintuitive, but handouts can bring greater attention to your main points and allow the audience to take notes. Fill-in-the-blank handouts seem most useful for keeping the audience fully engaged since they will have to follow along closely.

Three types of handouts are typically used in public speaking:

1. Printouts of your slides
2. Fill-in-the-blank handouts
3. An outline

In any case, there must be no typographical errors on your handout material, regardless of whether this is a class presentation, a briefing at work, or a presentation for a social setting. It comes across as though you rushed through your preparation and didn't put in the time to properly proofread and edit. This can turn off your audience and chip away at your credibility.

At a large event, you don't want to make the mistake of distributing the handout material yourself. This will cause delays and confusion before your presentation. The handout should be printed in the program book with other speakers' material or given out by the administrative team when participants register.

In cases where you have a lot of information to share with the audience, you might consider handing out a summary of your points and providing additional material on CDs, on flash drives, or by posting it to your website.

Design your handouts so that audiences are less likely to throw them away:

- Include important reference information on each page (websites, phone numbers, book titles), not all together on the last page that can be easily ripped out.
- Include checklists, quizzes, top ten lists, space for notes, and other things on important or personal topics as appropriate.
- Include a list of unique or memorable quotes in the handouts.

Handouts are not a substitute for a quality presentation!

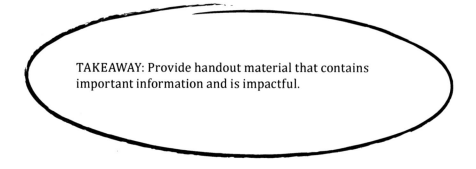

TAKEAWAY: Provide handout material that contains important information and is impactful.

Lesson 24

Dress for Success

You cannot climb the ladder of success dressed in the costume of failure.

~ Zig Ziglar

They expect a professional presentation, so they expect to see a 'professional.'
Dress appropriately for the occasion, but don't be one of the crowd.

~ Wess Roberts

Speakers address audiences in all manner of attire.

For some men, the rule of thumb is cut and dry: always wear a jacket and tie.

For some women, knee-length skirts or slacks with dress shirts or jackets are the norm.

At the other end of the spectrum, some wear blue jeans regardless of the audience.

For others still, their dress varies with the kind of audience they are facing.

When deciding how to dress for a speaking engagement, you need to consider a number of things, including:

- Who is the audience?

- What is the setting?

- What is the purpose of the event?

- What is your topic?

A conference held in a major city for lawyers or doctors will likely call for speakers to wear business attire, including ties for men and suits for men and women alike. If this same conference were held at a resort, business casual might be more appropriate.

A conference of entrepreneurs might call for speakers to dress in business casual. If these entrepreneurs are tech-related, you might expect to see much more casual dress, such as jeans and t-shirts or polo shirts.

Years ago, I spoke at a hotel across the street from a beach during the summer. The audience for the three-day conference was very casual, some in shorts, t-shirts, and even bikinis. I wore a full suit and tie. This proved to be distracting to the audience, and they let me know it.

On another occasion, I spoke at a retreat on a ranch. The audience was small and dressed in jeans, shorts, and t-shirts. I wore dress jeans (dark denim, straight-legged) and a button-down shirt. It worked perfectly.

You don't necessarily want to dress on the same level as the audience. By the same token, you don't want to be so many levels above your audience that you alienate them.

Pick out something that makes you feel powerful and confident but that doesn't come across as condescending or inappropriate. If unsure, have someone look over your attire prior to the presentation.

TAKEAWAY: Dress one notch above the audience without being distracting.

Record Your Presentation

*You were born to win, but to be a winner you must
plan to win, prepare to win, and expect to win.*

~ Zig Ziglar

*We gain strength, and courage, and confidence
by each experience in which we really stop to
look fear in the face. We must do that which we think
we cannot.*

~ Eleanor Roosevelt

One of the best ways to reduce nervousness, increase confidence, and improve your presentation is to record it.

You may be thinking, "I sound terrible on tape" or "I hate the way I look on video," and then resist recording yourself.

I know how you feel. I've always hated watching myself on video or listening to my recorded voice. But once you truly commit to recording yourself and honestly assessing it, the improvement in your presentation will be meteoric.

Recording is perhaps the single quickest and most effective way to face the brutal facts and make timely improvements.

Most important, assessing your recorded performance and making necessary changes will help you to quickly move off the plateau to the next leap of progress.

The first big public speaking engagement I had was a fundraiser before 250 people – and I was the featured speaker. In fact, I was the only speaker. And I was a nervous wreck!

Because I was so nervous, I spent a lot of time rehearsing. I wrote out my presentation and recorded it. Listened and analyzed, rewrote and re-recorded. The practice paid off, and the event was a hit.

There is no way I would have been able to judge my presentation without getting outside myself. I knew that the human mind has a great facility for justification, self-deception, and other tricks for ignoring faults and avoiding criticism.

While you're speaking, you can't fully gauge your voice, facial expressions, and gestures while also managing the content of your presentation and monitoring the audience – at least not without a lot of practice.

You may not be aware of nervous habits, that your posture is poor, or that you're gesturing too much (or not enough) with your hands.

Seeking out constructive criticism is one of the keys to success, and the recordings don't lie. For best results, record your presentations. This practice alone will take you to the next level in your speaking ability.

You may not realize it at the time, but as you are making, assessing, and perfecting your audio and video performances, you are also developing skills that may lead to producing electronic versions of your presentation. Providing (or even selling) CDs, DVDs, podcasts, or teleseminars is becoming more necessary in today's high-tech, information-driven world.

TAKEAWAY: Record your presentations as the best way to improve your public speaking as quickly as possible.

Part 3

The Presentation: Getting the Nerve

Know the Room

*It's not the will to win that matters – everyone has
that. It's the will to prepare to win that matters.*

~ Paul "Bear" Bryant

*Another way to be prepared is to think negatively.
Yes, I'm a great optimist. but, when trying to make a
decision, I often think of the worst case scenario. I call it
'the eaten by wolves factor.' If I do something, what's the
most terrible thing that could happen? Would I be eaten
by wolves? One thing that makes it possible to be an
optimist, is if you have a contingency plan for when all
hell breaks loose. There are a lot of things I don't worry
about, because I have a plan in place if they do.*

~ Randy Pausch

One great way to reduce fear and nervousness is to size up the actual meeting room before the event.

Arrive early to examine the setting. Walk the room and test the equipment. Note safety exits and fire extinguishers, restrooms, climate control, or whatever else you might need, and get comfortable with the lectern, microphone, stage, and aisles.

Know where the light switches are if you are showing slides or video.

- Does one button control the whole room?
- Are they dimmer lights?

- Will the entire room go pitch black with the flick of just one switch?
- Can you lower just the front lights to accent the screen better?

Once the room goes completely black, you will start losing your audience, especially if it's an afternoon presentation.

If you're using your own equipment, know where the outlets are and whether you will need an extension cord or power strip. A review of the room prior to the presentation will answer all of your questions.

- How many people will be in the audience?
- How large is the room?
- If the microphone stops working or the batteries die, will the audience still hear you, or will you have to wait for replacement equipment?

Think about speaking from the floor to get close to the audience, avoiding the lectern whenever possible. It will help you connect with the audience if there are no barriers between you and them.

If you're not the first speaker, try to watch the speaker before you. You can see how he or she is using the room. You will get a sense of the audience. You may be able to draw connections between your presentation and the previous one.

Once when I was speaking at a conference, the morning speaker had changed his topic without telling the conference organizer and ended up covering some of the material I was going to present. Since I had watched his presentation, I could adjust my material and avoid an embarrassing situation.

When you arrive at the location early enough, not only can you check all of the technical and logistical requirements for your presentation, you can also do a quick visualization exercise to let your brain experience your successful performance even before you get up to speak.

No one cares about your success more than you. Don't leave important details to chance. With details in hand, your fear and nervousness will decrease.

TAKEAWAY: Get comfortable with the meeting room so you're ready to focus on delivering a great presentation.

Your Pre-talk Psych Up

*Anything that loosens you up and makes you freer
is good, because that's what acting and performing
is all about – being free. It gives you a better
connection to the audience.*

~ Brett Somers

*When you concentrate your energy purposely on
the future possibility that you aspire to realize,
your energy is passed on to it and makes it attracted
to you with a force stronger than the one you
directed towards it.*

~ Stephen Richards

If you haven't realized it yet, when you engage in public speaking you're really in the entertainment business.

Every good performer knows the value and the necessity of getting in the right frame of mind before going in front of an audience.

And let's be clear: This applies regardless of who you are and who you are presenting to, whether you're a student presenting a paper in class, the best man making a toast at a wedding, an employee presenting to your department, a coach inspiring your team, or professional speaker talking with thousands of people.

As a novice speaker, you might use the following as an effective pre-talk psych up:

"I've prepared my heart out. I feel great, and I'll give it my best. I know that this is just the first of many presentations. I'm a sincere and genuine speaker. It doesn't have to be perfect."

If listening to energizing music psyches you up, by all means, go right ahead.

In your pre-talk psych up, repeat the visualization exercise that's become part of your confidence-building process: See how tall you're standing, how calm you feel, how well you're doing, and even how much fun you're having. When you get in front of the audience, your body will easily fall into this habit of feeling great since you have played it over and over in your mind already.

Your pre-talk psych up gets your energy and passion going. You can't expect an audience to get excited if you aren't. A smile on your face and great body language are indispensable tools in energizing an audience.

Interestingly enough, for me, speaking in front of an audience of 1,000 has been as easy as speaking in front of 20. The larger group provides me with a tremendous amount of energy, aiding me in my pre-talk psych up.

The most effective psych-up for me is when I engage the audience before the presentation. It gets my blood pumping and gives the audience a chance to relax and laugh a little.

If you can speak with the audience before you actually begin your presentation, it helps to calm your butterflies, warm up the audience, and build up their energy, too.

Your pre-talk psych up is all emotion. The technical part is done. You did your preparation thoroughly. You managed the details. You familiarized yourself with the room. You tested your equipment. Now comes the fun part, speaking!

TAKEAWAY: Develop rituals for turbocharging your passion before a presentation.

Lesson 28
Making the Delivery

It is delivery that makes the orator's success.

~ Johann Wolfgang von Goethe

I've been told to speed up my delivery when I perform. But if I lose the stammer, I'm just another slightly amusing accountant.

~ Bob Newhart

Your delivery is essentially the packaging you build up around your message.

If you think your message and content are the most important things, consider this: If you fail to create an effective delivery, your content will be lost. The audience will lose interest and your message will not get through.

What are important ways you can dress up your content?

Don't forget important aspects of your delivery that are discussed elsewhere, like dressing for success (Lesson 24), writing your own introduction (Lesson 29), using humor (Lesson 37), understanding the pitfalls of the lectern (Lesson 39) and the microphone (Lesson 40), and the flow of your presentation (Lesson 21).

There are two key aspects of delivery that require your close attention.

First and foremost is your voice. You're excited to be with the audience. Show it! The passion in your voice will help keep the audience interested.

Modulate your voice as necessary, using higher and lower pitch as effectively as possible. When telling stories, use different voices to "act out" the various characters you portray.

In my programs, I tell a dramatic story involving an 80-year-old woman with a Queens, New York, accent. Only after I began mimicking her voice and inserting dramatic pauses did audiences really start responding to the story. Everybody enjoys a good story that is told well.

Second, your body language will betray any negative feelings or misgivings you have about being in front of the audience.

Your eyes and smile as well as your posture will give you away. The audience will notice if your voice and gestures are out of sync. A well-modulated voice should be accompanied by appropriate varying body language. And don't forget to smile.

Be aware of your hands. I knew a speaker who, every ten seconds or so, would clap his hands together. I don't know if he was aware of it, but the audience surely was.

Years ago, in my early days of speaking, I would rock back and forth during my presentation. Fortunately, a friend of mine was in the audience once and told me about it.

You will make a lot of adjustments as you gain confidence speaking. But be vigilant about these basic dynamics of speaking. They will make a huge difference.

TAKEAWAY: Let your voice and body language work with you to show that you're comfortable in front of the group.

Your Introduction

*Do you suppose I could buy back
my introduction to you?*

~ Groucho Marx

*What we say is important...for in most cases the
mouth speaks what the heart is full of.*

~ Jim Beggs

It is very easy to overlook the value of writing your own introduction. But as a public speaker in any setting, you should appreciate that the audience wants to know who you are and why you are the one speaking to them on that particular topic.

Understand which occasions will require an introduction and in which ones you can introduce yourself.

If you are working with a program organizer and send him or her your biographical information, résumé, or curriculum vitae with the expectation that he or she will extract the appropriate highlights and give you the best introduction for that occasion, you are likely to be disappointed.

There are two critical things to remember:

1. Program organizers will be extremely busy with countless other details.

    The organizer will not have time to edit your bio or wade through your résumé to find out how wonderful you are, how many awards you have won, or if you like alpine skiing. It's also likely that the organizer won't know exactly how best to represent you. Program organizers may or may not be subject matter experts. In many cases, they are logistics and support personnel.

2. You are the person who cares the most about your presentation.

    Your reputation is on the line every time you get up to speak. Since you've done some research about the occasion, the audience, and the host organization, you know best how to highlight your background to address their needs.

When you write your own introduction for a formal public speaking occasion, you:

- Control the impression being generated about you even before you stand up
- Minimize the surprises that could arise in the course of an introduction
- Signal to the organizer that you are organized, thoughtful, and easy to work with – ingredients that help get you invited to speak again
- Save the organizer a lot of time

If appropriate, you will also have an opportunity to say a few more words about your background in the course of your presentation.

It can be very effective if you can relate to the audience how your own experiences informed your knowledge of the topic at hand. This helps to enhance the connection between you and the audience.

TAKEAWAY: Write your own introduction highlighting the most important information that the audience should hear.

Lesson 30
Strong Out of the Gate

Start with a bang!

~ Rob Sherman

Be still when you have nothing to say; when genuine passion moves you, say what you've got to say, and say it hot.

~ D. H. Lawrence

So, you have done all of your planning, researching, writing, and rehearsing. You've communicated with the teacher, program organizer, your boss, or whoever is coordinating the event at which you're speaking.

The big day has arrived; you feel good and have gone through your pre-talk psych up. You're good to go. The host just introduced you.

And now you stand up to start your compelling presentation with passion and energy.

"Hello, my name is Pete Smith. I'm happy to be here. Thank you for that warm introduction. What a wonderful looking audience. Can you hear me in the back? Is this thing working?"

You call that passion and energy?

That's not very compelling or genuine. Why tell them what they already know? Why check a microphone you checked during your preparation?

When a TV show fails to capture our attention in the first minute or two, we frequently turn the channel. Fortunately, audiences don't get up and walk out of live presentations in the first two minutes. But they will switch off their attention very quickly if you don't get them engaged.

The audience wants to know: WIIFM – What's In It For Me?

Start with a challenging question, a startling statistic, an interesting quote, or a surprising news headline. Any of these is better than the tired, worn openings the audience members have heard at the beginning of every other presentation they've attended.

But ... beware of starting out with a joke (Lesson 37).

In my time management program, the first thing I say is, "How would your life change if you had an extra hour every day?"

This signals that I'm here to talk about them, not me, and my presentation will be personally valuable to each and every attendee. I have their attention. By opening this way, I'm promising I will not be wasting their time.

When starting a program this way, I'm also signaling to them that I'm prepared. I give them a sense that they're about to embark on a journey. I intimate that I have discovered something that will be useful to them that they can apply in their lives.

I start addressing WIIFM from the very first sentence.

TAKEAWAY: Grab the audience from the very first sentence and give them a reason to go on a journey with you.

Lesson 31

Break the Ice

*It is good to break the ice by some whose words are
of less weight, and to reserve
the more weighty voice to come in as by chance.*

~ Francis Bacon

*Fie, fie upon her! There's language in her eye, her
cheek, her lip, Nay, her foot speaks; her wanton
spirits look out At every joint and motive of her body.*

~ William Shakespeare

People can be shy, hesitant, and careful until they sense that the environment they're in is safe and those around them mean them no harm. It's similar with public speaking.

Once the audience realizes you have personality, you enjoy engaging with them, and you put them at ease, they will give back to you.

Unfortunately, many speakers signal with their body language, voicing, and introduction that it's just going to be another boring presentation. Without breaking the ice it may take some time to get the audience relaxed and on your side. But if you're only speaking for an hour, that is valuable time lost.

Here are four quick ways to break the ice:

1. Warm up.

Talk with the audience in advance of your presentation if possible, perhaps as they are filing into the room. This is akin to opening acts that warm up an audience before the main attraction. It loosens people up, increases the energy, and changes the dynamics of the room (Lesson 17).

2. Have props.

    Just the presence of props in the room, if they are big enough to be visible from the audience, can set a different tone and increase the energy. Of course, this won't work if you have a magic trick that involves the nickel in your pocket (Lesson 33).

3. Bring humor.

    A joke can help break the ice, but only if you are a skilled joke-teller. Speakers usually aren't great at that. Instead, find ways to infuse humor naturally throughout your presentation. An additional advantage of humor over joke-telling is that the audience won't learn anything about you from a single joke, but they can from your humor (Lesson 37).

4. Body language.

    People want to be part of a winning team, something bigger than themselves. When they see the speaker as open, active, and happy to be there, they are ready to pay attention and see what happens next (Lesson 28).

Breaking the ice is such a critical part of public speaking. Remember, the audience wants to be entertained, informed, and persuaded. But in order for them to get what they came for, you have to do your best to put them in the proper frame of mind.

TAKEAWAY: Building a connection is about engaging the audience as quickly and genuinely as possible through the use of props, body language, and expressions of your personality.

Lesson 32

Let the Audience Know About You

*Don't introduce me to that man! I want to go on
hating him, and I can't hate a man whom I know.*

~ Charles Lamb

*Live your life from your heart. Share from
your heart. And your story will touch and heal
people's souls.*

~ Melody Beattie

Just as it's important to know something about the audience, the audience wants to know something about you. They want to understand where you've come from and how you qualify to stand before them.

The audience will learn something about you through four main avenues:

1. Promotional material announcing your presentation

2. How you are introduced at the event

3. Additional information you share during your remarks (especially personal stories, examples of success, and lessons learned)

4. How you present yourself (punctuality, attire, speech, tone, and so on)

Every audience loves stories and likes to be entertained.

Some of the connection between you and the audience may come from personal stories about your childhood, school, or travel.

You might decide to share mistakes you made and what you learned. This makes you real to them.

It's easier for the audience to make a connection with someone they see as real, fallible, and human.

At the same time, the audience wants to feel that you have achieved something noteworthy, have solved a problem, or have valuable insight that helps them in some way.

What you tell about yourself should be somehow related to the topic. You don't need to say a lot, but a few words about your experience with the topic and an appropriate story to share more about yourself works well. This is true whether the presentation is informational or inspirational.

Telling the audience something about you enhances the conversation. As you are telling your stories, sharing your mistakes, or making them laugh, the audience is thinking about how your experience applies in their lives.

Some public speaking trainers claim there is no place for personal stories in the course of a presentation. While one has to consider the topic and the audience, this is not great advice.

It's more difficult to make a connection with speakers who don't say anything about themselves.

TAKEAWAY: Strengthen the connection between you and your audience by sharing something about yourself when appropriate.

Lesson 33

Using Props to Make the Connection

I use many props. The props act as cue cards reminding me of what to say next.

~ Tom Ogden

Acting is all about big hair and funny props.... All the great actors knew it. Olivier knew it, Brando knew it.

~ Harold Ramis

One of the best ways to connect with the audience is to be different from every other speaker.

Boring presentations and bad PowerPoints are a dime a dozen.

Remember, people want to be entertained.

What can you do that's appropriate for the presentation and gives the audience more than they expect? Use props.

Props change the atmosphere of a presentation:

- Having props at the front of the room signals to the audience that they're about to experience something different. Their energy level will be higher.

- Frequently, participants will speculate about the props with each other before the presentation begins. In some measure, this helps break the ice and creates a relaxed environment.

- Props help reach more of the audience than if you rely only on the spoken word. Visual, auditory, and kinesthetic learners will get more out of your presentation.

- Props help breathe new life into a topic the audience may have heard countless times. Suddenly, they are thinking about the material in a new way thanks to your creativity.

I have found effective ways to use the harmonica and guitar to illustrate points in my presentations on time management, effective communication, emotional intelligence, and leadership.

I can assure you that virtually no one in the audience has ever seen a speaker play the harmonica during a program.

Using a prop can enhance your connection with the audience, energize them after lunch, and make your presentation memorable.

In addition, it helps relax the room and reduce your fear and nervousness.

Handout material, name tags, table tents, gift pens, and door prizes are just some basic props that help the audience feel welcome and appreciated.

The right props underscore the great points you're already making and bring an additional dimension to them, but they should never be a substitute or a distraction.

TAKEAWAY: Use appropriate props to increase audience attention and to get your message across more effectively.

Lesson 34

Quotes, Poems, Songs, Books, and Movies

Literature adds to reality, it does not simply describe it. It enriches the necessary competencies that daily life requires and provides; and in this respect, it irrigates the deserts that our lives have already become.

~ C.S. Lewis

Poems and songs penned as an unstoppable outpouring of the heart take on a life of their own. They transcend the limits of nationality and time as they pass from person to person, from one heart to another.

~ Daisaku Ikeda

The methods open to you to infuse creativity into your public speaking are limited only by your imagination.

You should be thinking about every resource at your disposal to get your point across, including quotes, poems, songs, books, and movies.

The arts touch the heart and soul, and that's what your audience came for – to learn something, to feel something, to have an experience.

What better resource for a presentation than literature and music?

Often, poets and artists express the sentiments we're searching for more effectively, more economically, and more elegantly than we ever could, so by all means use them to reach your audience.

It's about the connection.

After you've made the connection, you want to take the audience on a journey, conveying to them what's possible.

Intertwining your message with powerful poems, songs, and quotes when appropriate can be a potent tool for inspiring your audience.

When you use the various forms of art in the context of your unique experience to illustrate your point, you can move the audience to say, "I never thought of it that way!"

That's a profound moment, and you just might trigger responses in them that will change their perspective and maybe even their lives.

You also lend authority to your presentation when you quote someone, especially if it is a citation of a well-known, respected individual. You are supporting your argument with evidence of its "rightness."

In my time management program, we discuss setting and reaching goals, focus, discipline, and other important components of success. The classic clip from *The Karate Kid* movie where Mr. Miyagi is instructing Daniel LaRusso on the finer points of "Wax on, wax off" is a fun surprise for the audience and gets the point across.

At the end of your program, especially if it's an inspirational or motivational one, you should issue a call to action when appropriate and leave the audience inspired.

Instead of ending programs on a flat note, wrap up your presentation with a personal story and the verses of a song or a poem to *inspire* the audience to take action.

After all, that's what it's all about.

TAKEAWAY: Engaging, impactful, inspirational material for your presentations is all around you. Stretch your imagination to find something that will connect with the audience.

Lesson 35

Stay on Message

Without discipline there is no life at all.

~ Katherine Hepburn

Every speaker has a mouth;
An arrangement rather neat.
Sometimes it's filled with wisdom.
Sometimes it's filled with feet.

~ Robert Orben

Once you know the central theme of your presentation, stick to it!

Everything you talk about must contribute to the main points you're trying to make.

When you start veering off course, you may not find your way back.

The audience can become confused, and you may lose their attention.

It's tempting to use stories, props, and humor in your presentation to show how clever you are or if you think they will paint you in a positive light.

But if they don't support your overall message and serve the audience's needs, they must be removed from the presentation.

Many years ago, I got a coveted speaking engagement at an upscale New York City hotel to an audience of very successful Wall Street investment bankers and attorneys.

Sometime during my preparation, I got it in my mind that I would show a short film I had produced. But the film was not central to my message. It went over with an embarrassing thud.

Remember the cardinal rule: It's *always* about the audience.

The best way to stay on message is to begin with the end in mind: Understand your audience and know what you would like to achieve.

For short events, like a brief speech, an outline will keep you on track. In that setting, you are not likely to make many impromptu remarks.

For short events, don't try to cover too much material, and don't rush through your presentation. You only increase the chances of getting flustered and losing your way.

For longer events, like presentations or training programs several hours in duration, take a break to collect your thoughts when you feel the need to regroup.

If you take questions during your presentation, be sure to have a way to get back on track, like limiting the number of consecutive questions you take at any given time.

Once, I made the mistake of trying to answer questions that were not directly on the topic of the presentation. I got off track, lost valuable time, and had to leave out important information. Additionally, some audience members were annoyed that I spent time answering those questions.

Concentrating on your message and being comfortable with your tools to stay on message helps reduce fear and anxiety about presenting.

TAKEAWAY: Don't stray from the main theme of your presentation or you risk confusing your audience.

Lesson 36
Eliminate Verbal Fillers

*You can speak well if your tongue can deliver the
message of your heart.*

~ John Ford

*Eloquence, at its highest pitch, leaves little room
for reason or reflection, but addresses itself entirely
to the desires and affections, captivating the willing
hearers, and subduing their understanding.*

~ David Hume

You may think that "ums" and "uhs" buy you thinking time during your presentation. Maybe you think the "likes" and "you knows" are just part of the normal flow of speech.

Actually, these words and phrases (called vocalized pauses or verbal fillers) add nothing to the content of your presentation. What's worse, they actually take away from your remarks. Audience members may find your fillers distracting and irritating.

Recall a speaker who used "ums," "uhs," "like," "basically," "actually," or similar meaningless repetitions to the point of distraction. In high school, I had a teacher who said "fellas" constantly. My friends and I counted more than 300 "fellas" in one class period, but we missed most of what he said.

Fillers and other inappropriate pauses have to be filtered out of your presentation by your audience. They weaken your credibility and you may be perceived as lacking preparation, knowledge, and passion.

There are several ways to reduce verbal fillers:

Notice when other people use "ums," "uhs," "likes," and "you knows" when they talk. Realize that these words are not contributing to the conversation. Make a commitment to drive them out of your daily speech.

Record or videotape your presentation to check your speaking style for verbal fillers. This will increase your awareness of the problem and help you to break the habit.

Understand why you are doing it. Are you nervous? Unprepared? Do you believe these fillers are giving the audience the perception that you are actually thinking on the spot?

Raise your level of preparation. The best way to drive down the use of verbal fillers is to prepare and rehearse and then rehearse some more.

Slow down. You might be using these fillers if you think you should be talking all the time. Getting comfortable with pauses is a great way to improve your presentation, and you won't be rushing to fill every second in front of a room with talking (Lesson 43).

Monitor your progress and be patient.

These steps will help you become more aware of your verbal fillers, anticipate them while you're speaking, and drive them out of your presentation style.

I'll keep repeating it: It's always about the audience. Verbal fillers do nothing to serve anyone.

TAKEAWAY: Eliminating verbal fillers will help the audience stay engaged and make you look better prepared.

Lesson 37

Find the Funny Bone

Laugh as much as possible, always laugh. It's the sweetest thing one can do for oneself and one's fellow human beings.

~ Maya Angelou

The joke must be funny in itself, get a great delivery, and fit the audience and situation.
That's a difficult trifecta for most amateur presenters   to pull off.

~ Dave Zielinski

It's frequently said that opening a presentation with a joke helps break the ice. That may be true, but it's a strategy fraught with danger. I don't recommend it.

Here are just a few of the potential pitfalls:

- The audience may have heard the joke before (or a thousand times before).

- The audience may not have the same sense of humor as you and may not get it.

- The joke may take on a different meaning in their line of work or may simply be in bad taste.

- They might laugh at it in a social setting but not at a presentation.

- You may come across as canned or trying too hard if comedy is not your forté.

Ask yourself: "If this joke goes badly, is it worth alienating the audience, torpedoing my self-confidence, and undermining the rest of my presentation?" "Am I telling a joke to show how clever I am, or is it for the benefit of the audience?"

If your presentation requires the audience to laugh at your joke and they don't, you lose – big time.

There is a difference between telling jokes and using humor. Know yourself and your abilities in order to find the best approach for you and your audience.

I know that I'm a horrible joke-teller, so I never even consider telling one. The thought of delivering a joke successfully would distract me from the rest of my material.

Instead, I rely on my ability to use what's happening in the room to create impromptu humorous moments. I also use photos, wacky images, and stories to nudge the audience's funny bone.

In one of my presentations, I show three pictures of me in elementary school. On the way to making my point, I say, "I don't hold any grudges against my mother for these hairstyles." Invariably, the crowd laughs. In this way, I don't need to worry about telling jokes and can still keep the atmosphere light.

Leslie Brunker, a consultant who helps trainers extract more humor from their sessions, says, "Fun and play are not always what we make happen, but what we *allow* to happen."

TAKEAWAY: Think about other forms of humor than telling a joke if you are not a seasoned joke-teller.

Lesson 38

Managing the Room

A man is hindered and distracted in proportion as he draws outward things to himself.

~ Thomas a Kempis

It's easier for a rich man to ride that camel through the eye of a needle directly into the Kingdom of Heaven, than for some of us to give up our cell phone.

~ Vera Nazaria

As with any group that comes together to listen to a presentation, your audience may be a source of distractions and interruptions: people walk in late, cell phones ring, audience members whisper to each other during your talk.

It is important to manage the room you're speaking in. This is particularly the case if you are the host of your own event or you're the sole speaker at an event. Here are some useful tips:

Ask the audience to check their cell phones, put them on vibrate, or turn them off. In many cases, audience members may need to take a phone call. Announce at the beginning that they're welcome to step out of the room to do so.

Alternatively, if appropriate, you could ask the audience to make sure their cell phones are on and that they should feel welcome to tweet or post to Facebook anything of interest that they hear you, the speaker, say.

Be ready to go at the appointed time, especially if you are not the host of the event. If you're the host, it is still desirable to be punctual, but the atmosphere may be a little more casual and relaxed. Use your best judgment depending on circumstances.

Observe your time limit. It is better to end a little bit earlier and have the audience wanting more than to finish late. By the same token, if you have a lot of material remaining toward the end of your presentation, make a decision about what needs to be skipped in order to finish on time.

But be certain not to sacrifice your strong finish. This is one of the things the audience will remember most.

If you're speaking for more than 90 minutes, you will need to consider taking one or more breaks, depending on the total length of your speaking time. Be attuned to the audience. If they're getting fidgety, it's time for a break.

Ensure to the extent possible that there is no extraneous noise just outside the room where you're speaking. I've asked maintenance crews to delay their work outside meeting rooms and speakers in adjoining meeting rooms in hotel settings to lower the volume of their video presentations if they interfered with my presentations.

Have whatever materials you need for your presentation at the front of the room with you and easily accessible. All of my props, supplies, backup equipment – anything I may need to access during my presentation – are set up in advance and at hand when I need them.

TAKEAWAY: Know the dynamics of the room and your audience and do your best to influence them in a positive way, minimizing distractions.

The Problem of the Lectern

The human brain starts working the moment
you are born and never stops until you
stand up to speak in public.

~ George Jessel

There can be no vulnerability without risk;
there can be no community without vulnerability;
there can be no peace, and ultimately no life,
without community.

~ M. Scott Peck

The temptation is great to think of a lectern as a protector, as a place to hide trembling legs. However, the audience will still notice every detail about your presence behind a lectern.

Actually, as a barrier, a lectern makes it more difficult for you to connect with the audience. It's ideal if there is nothing standing between you and the audience, but if you have to use one, make the best of it.

All too often, speakers begin to speak almost before they are settled in front of the microphone. When you step up to the lectern, take time to make it your own.

Adjust the microphone as needed. If there's an on/off switch, turn the microphone off before moving it. The microphone should not cover your mouth.

Have a glass of water set out before speaking. If there's not one there, take a second to pour yourself a glass before speaking.

If you are using a script or notes of any kind, make sure your papers or note cards are together and ready for you to start speaking. If they aren't, take a second to bring order to your material.

Get settled in the space and take a second to look at your audience. This is your way of acknowledging their presence. Don't worry about a second or two of quiet time.

If the only microphone you're using is on the lectern, don't turn away from it while you're speaking. If you're using PowerPoint, don't turn toward the screen to talk about something in your slide. The audience will not hear you. Consider adjusting the angle or location of the lectern so that looking at or pointing to the screen doesn't pull you away from the microphone.

Be sure to keep your head and eyes up. To help you do this, keep your notes or speech (if you're reading one) at the top of the lectern so that you're not looking directly downward to read.

Keep your body four-to-six inches from the lectern. You shouldn't be leaning on or against the lectern; you want to be visible to the audience and make connecting with them as easy as possible.

Resist the urge to grasp the side of the lectern for dear life or drum your fingers out of nervousness. You want to look comfortable and natural.

If you have the opportunity and it's appropriate, begin speaking at the lectern and then move out from behind it to continue your comments, eliminating the barrier between you and the audience. You will need to make sure you have a wireless lavaliere microphone attached to you, of course (unless the room is very small).

TAKEAWAY: Only use a lectern if absolutely necessary and practice using it effectively.

Lesson 40

Step Up to the Mic

*Despite all the technical improvements, it still boils
down to a man or a woman and a microphone,
playing music, sharing stories, talking about issues –
communicating with an audience.*

~ Casey Kasem

*I found at an early age the times when I learned
the most about myself was when I got thrown
out there on a stage in front of a microphone when
you didn't really want to be out there, where
you're kind of afraid.*

~ Andrew Shue

The microphone can be the single source of countless aggravations for a speaker. It can feed back. It can be too loud or too low. It can be in the wrong position. The batteries can die.

You must use a microphone unless you truly have a very strong voice or you're speaking to a small group. You will lose your audience if they can't hear you clearly.

Don't blow into the microphone to test it. Don't begin your presentation with, "Can you hear me back there?" or "Is this thing on?" This is a weak beginning, and, if you're the first or only speaker, you should've already tested it for volume.

In your prepping, you found out if the microphone has an on/off switch or a mute switch. Sometimes you may be required to turn on the microphone yourself, especially a lavaliere (wireless lapel microphone), before you speak, and mute it during a break.

The organizers of the program (if applicable) should have put fresh batteries in the microphone. You may consider bringing some with you to the presentation, just in case. AAA batteries seem to be the most common.

Make adjustments to the microphone before you start speaking. If it's possible to make adjustments before the audience is present, or if you can turn it off before making adjustments, so much the better.

I always prefer a lavaliere because it gives me the independence to move around and to get closer to the audience. With that said, here are some things to look out for:

- Be careful to always speak through the microphone when turning to address someone to your right or left. Oftentimes, speakers turn their heads too far in either direction to make a comment and most of the audience can't hear it. This is particularly true when speaking at a lectern.

- Be aware that sometimes lavalieres can slip or get turned around if they are not fastened properly. As a result, the audio quality will suffer.

- Be careful with the placement of the microphone. If it's too close to your mouth, the Ps and Bs at the beginning of words will explode with an irritating sound. A lavaliere will pick up a lot of sounds like rustling of papers, your jacket, your starched collar, and jewelry.

- Be conscious that if you're emphasizing a point about yourself, you may be tempted to point to yourself or pat your chest. It will boom in a lavaliere mic if you accidentally hit it.

- And don't forget to turn the lavaliere off or switch it to mute if you go to the restroom!

TAKEAWAY: Use preparation time to become familiar with the microphone. It can make or break your presentation.

No Apologies at the Start

The only correct actions are those that demand no explanation and no apology.

~ Red Auerbach

A stiff apology is a second insult.... The injured party does not want to be compensated because he has been wronged; he wants to be healed because he has been hurt.

~ Gilbert K. Chesterton

We know that the best way to capture an audience is to begin strongly out of the gate with a compelling story, a startling statistic, or a shocking headline. The audience has come for an experience, something meaningful.

You can easily imagine the impact on the audience when a speaker leads with one of the following openings:

- "I'm sorry I'm so late. The hotel forgot to give me a wake-up call."

- "Traffic getting here was a killer this morning. That's why I'm late."

- "Unfortunately, I was asked to give this speech at the last minute, so I'm not very well prepared."

- "I would have liked to have shown you some videos today, but there was an equipment failure."

When you open with such statements, you set the tone for the rest of the presentation. You have set the audience up with negative energy. They already know you were late or the equipment doesn't work. There is no need to remind them of it.

When you apologize about things like traffic, you are simply saying that you did not respect the audience enough to plan properly.

When you apologize in the way indicated above, you have blamed everyone and everything but yourself for the situation. You are protecting your own ego...and it shows. You run the risk of undermining everything you're about to say in your presentation.

The need to apologize is minimized by following basic advice given throughout this book.

- Begin with the end in mind.

- Put first things first.

- Leave in plenty of time to get there in plenty of time.

- Plan the work and work the plan.

And when something goes wrong – which it will – put your best foot forward under the circumstances in which you find yourself (Lesson 45).

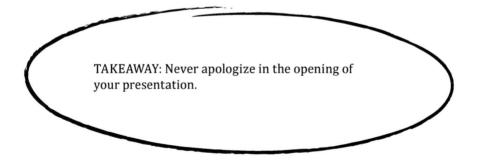

TAKEAWAY: Never apologize in the opening of your presentation.

Lesson 42

The Eyes Have It

Insincerity is always weakness; sincerity even in error is strength.

~ George Henry Lewes

The eyes are the most powerful social signalers that we have and hence are sometimes called 'the windows of the soul.' One of the key elements of what is called 'social skills training' is getting just the right amount of eye contact.

~ Glen Wilson

The use of your eyes in a presentation is one of your best tools in connecting with the audience.

Effective eye contact tells your audience several things:

- You're sincere

- You're interested in them

- You're confident and prepared

- You're knowledgeable

- You're trustworthy

Stare too long and you risk losing your audience. It's very useful to identify audience members who smile, look friendly, and are seemingly receptive to your message. Noticing these people in the audience can reduce nervousness in a presentation, but address only them and you risk alienating the rest.

Dart your eyes and you risk coming across as insincere. The opposite practice can also present a problem. If you are trying to address everyone in a large room at the same time, your eyes will be shifting back and forth so much that you will come across as insincere and untrustworthy.

Work a large audience in segments. Use the center as your main segment and then shift to address the left side of the room and make a point. Then deliver a point to the right side of the room and then back to center.

Use eye contact to monitor audience receptivity and reaction. Are they interested? Are they in agreement? Are they frowning or shaking their heads? Is now a good time for a break or maybe a Q&A period would be in order?

You may need to make adjustments to your presentation based on what you're seeing. If you are reading from a script, notes, or presentation, you may be oblivious to the reaction and needs of the audience.

If you are unaware of the audience's general reaction to you, then you are not communicating with them, and you're not allowing them to communicate with you. Public speaking is a conversation.

At the beginning of your public speaking experience, you may want to focus on the foreheads of the audience members, looking just over their heads, or picking a spot on the wall at the back of the room as ways to reduce nervousness. But move to eye contact as soon as possible. It will enhance the connection.

TAKEAWAY: Your job is to be sincere, authentic, passionate, and inspiring. Your eyes will show all of that and more.

Lesson 43

The Power of the Pause

*Vary the prose. Vary the pitch. Always remember
the pause.*

~ Winston Churchill

*The right word may be effective, but no word was
ever as effective as a rightly timed pause.*

~ Mark Twain

Before you get comfortable speaking, you may think that a pause, even just three seconds long, can be torture. Count it out. 1, 2, 3. With 20 or 50 or 200 sets of eyes staring at you, the silence can be unnerving and seem an eternity.

But that's not the way it is in reality.

Inexperienced speakers rush because they're excited. They rush because they're nervous. They rush because the presentation is going badly.

When you've prepared thoroughly, you want the audience to hear every word. You want to get nuances across. You speak clearly and take your time. And you use pauses as a conscious part of your speech.

In many cases, pauses are planned. They aren't awkward, unexpected, panic-inducing mistakes because, say, you've forgotten your script.

Pauses are a result of good preparation.

They can be used to build drama and excitement. They can be used for emphasis; they help to distinguish a vital piece of information from the rest of your program.

You use a pause because you know what's coming next. And what's coming next is something that will be meaningful to the audience.

You may think you have to talk constantly in order to keep the audience awake. You may be tempted to fill every pause with a verbal filler like "um" or "ah." But it is your ideas, your vocal inflection and intonation, and your dramatic use of pauses that will keep them awake, not your ability to fill time.

Pauses provide the time audiences need to catch up to what you're saying, absorb it, process it, and keep them open to what you're going to tell them next.

Pauses – without verbal fillers – are a great tool to create some valuable thinking time for yourself to quickly determine the direction ahead. This may seem unlikely now, but after you gain experience speaking, and when you know your topic inside and out, you will use pauses often to think on your feet.

Since you've practiced, rehearsed, and delivered, you know it's going to work. And since you've come to your audience with sincerity and authenticity, they know you are being heartfelt.

TAKEAWAY: Practice building pauses into your presentation to make powerful points.

Lesson 44

Make Mistakes

The greatest mistake you can make in life is to be continually fearing you will make one.

~ Elbert Hubbard

A smart man makes a mistake, learns from it, and never makes that mistake again. But a wise man finds a smart man and learns from him how to avoid the mistake altogether.

~ Roy H. Williams

The fear of making mistakes is perhaps the single most influential psychological dynamic in our lives. It keeps us from venturing beyond our comfort zone. It keeps us from learning and growing.

The fear of making mistakes lies at the core of the fear of public speaking. To be more precise, it is the response to our mistakes that we fear.

We fear misspeaking or drawing a blank in front of the audience. We fear embarrassing ourselves or offending someone. We fear not being able to measure up to others' expectations. We fear not being worthy enough of acceptance and love.

The fact is, we can't learn anything or improve at anything without making mistakes. But, we need to stop thinking of mistakes as faults, obstacles, and shortcomings, and start thinking of them as necessary bridges to success.

Audiences are very forgiving if you come prepared and perform with sincerity and authenticity. They will not forgive lack of preparation or half-hearted performance.

You are more attuned to the smallest details of your presentation than the audience is. What you consider a mistake, audiences frequently don't even notice.

In many cases, when you lose your train of thought, the audience will help you get back on track.

Once you realize that mistakes are not abstract but stem from very specific actions, it becomes far easier to identify them, acknowledge them, and correct them.

The more I spoke and the better I got, the easier it was to improvise, to bridge mistakes, to double back and blaze a new path. Most of the time, the audience didn't notice, and if they noticed, they didn't care much about it.

Many times, I discovered something from my mistake that I wouldn't have if I had strictly followed the script.

Once you have mastered the basics of public speaking, mistakes become opportunities to venture somewhere you hadn't before and to learn something new.

Prepare yourself as much as possible and get up in front of an audience. After your presentation, review your performance. If possible, solicit critique through evaluations or recordings of your presentation. Make your changes and speak again.

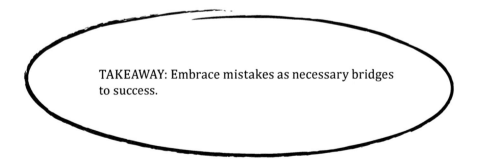

TAKEAWAY: Embrace mistakes as necessary bridges to success.

Lesson 45

When Things Go Wrong: Antidotes to Murphy's Law

Things turn out best for those who make the best of the way things turn out.

~ Jack Buck

My great concern is not whether you have failed, but whether you are content with your failure.

~ Abraham Lincoln

The best way to counter fear and nervousness is to be very well prepared.

Part of that preparation is envisioning what could go wrong and doing everything possible to mitigate the chances of that happening. But, let's face it, things go wrong.

Here are ten pointers for getting through a tough situation:

1. The very first thing you can control when things go wrong is your reaction to them.
2. Choose your response to things going wrong and rehearse it in your mind long before you get in front of the audience.
3. Understand in advance that you must be prepared to do your presentation without a computer, projector, or your PowerPoint. Sometimes technical issues just happen.

4. Do not panic. It doesn't contribute to the solution and undermines your leadership skills.

5. Keep your sense of humor. If your computer doesn't start, you can say, "I didn't feel like getting up this morning and apparently my laptop didn't either."

6. Don't play the blame game. It's a waste of time and the audience will see that you're preoccupied with your own ego. Your presentation is about them, not about you.

7. Do not continually refer to the problem. Everyone is already aware that something has gone wrong. Audiences are forgiving, but reminding them of the issue will not go over well.

8. Quickly assess the situation. Can you finish your presentation without resolving the issue? If it will take more than a few minutes to fix, let the audience take a break if appropriate.

9. Decide what assets and contacts you have available. Do you have the necessary items with you? Are you speaking at a hotel, company, or organization that can assist? Are there stores nearby?

10. The way you respond to the situation will go a long way in influencing how the audience thinks about your program overall.

Once when I was speaking, the batteries in the laptop remote control died. Since I always travel with batteries, this was no problem. I changed them while continuing to talk. People in the audience understood what was happening and later said, "Wow, you're really prepared."

TAKEAWAY: Never lose your temper or your sense of humor when something goes wrong.

Lesson 46

Managing Questions and Answers

Questions are never indiscreet,
answers sometimes are.

~ Oscar Wilde

Watch carefully when accomplished communicators
are handed a question. You will see them take a
few seconds to organize their thoughts before giving
a carefully constructed answer.

~ Richard Zeoli

The use of question-and-answer segments will depend on the type of presentation you are delivering.

A formal speech, keynote address, and comedy routine are not typically the kinds of presentations at which questions are asked.

If you plan to build a question-and-answer segment into your presentation, here are some tips to manage it successfully:

Entertain a question only if it is directly related to the topic being discussed.

If it doesn't quite fit your subject matter, either ask the audience member to ask it again later when discussing the specific topic or politely indicate that you can discuss it after the program.

Repeat the question. The audience will stop listening or start calling out, "Repeat the question!" if they can't hear.

Also, when you repeat the question accurately, the audience member who asked it will start nodding his or head in agreement. In other words, they are already poised to agree with your answer even before you've given it.

If you answer a question, don't allow yourself to get sidetracked. Stay on message.

One way to avoid straying off the main topic is to limit the number of questions you entertain at any given time. Take two or three questions and move on. You can repeat that later in the program if necessary.

It's OK to say, "I don't know." If you can't provide an answer later, tell them the most likely place they might find it or post it on your website. Audience members have thanked me for not pretending to know everything.

If allowing questions, be sure to entertain them *before* your closing. Closing a session with a question-and-answer segment runs the risk of a controversial or dull ending, especially if the questions are contentious or you can't answer them well. That will give what may have been a resounding presentation an unpredictable finish.

Question-and-answer segments are great opportunities to show off your sense of humor and get audiences to participate during a public speaking engagement.

Your closing will be used to issue a call to action, urging the audience to do something with the valuable information you just provided. Be sure that your question-and-answer segment doesn't run so long you can't do a proper closing.

TAKEAWAY: Entertain questions as appropriate, but don't get sidetracked. Never close your presentation with a question-and-answer segment.

Lesson 47

Finish Strong:
Close with InspirACTion

What you do makes a difference, and you have to decide what kind of difference you want to make.

~ Jane Goodall

Remember today, for it is the beginning of always.
Today marks the start of a brave new future
filled with all your dreams can hold.
Think truly to the future and make those dreams
come true.

~ Walter Winchell

Your presentation has gone great, and you're excited!

You opened up strongly, included some light material where appropriate; moved to the core of your message; developed it; made an argument; and hopefully informed, persuaded, and entertained your audience.

You have been delivering your presentation with passion and sincerity, sharing your expertise in a compelling way with stories, photos, videos, and humor, if the situation called for it.

Now it's time to wrap up, but closing in a boring way undermines all of your effort.

Audience members will readily remember the last thing you tell them. Make it special.

Whether you're helping your audience to lose weight, calling for increased productivity at work, or even delivering an academic paper at a conference, your ultimate goal is to present your compelling information and close in a way that inspires audience members to *act*.

You can offer guidance on the best tools and approaches available to affect change. You can talk about how you were able to improve your own situation dramatically. You could even recommend policy changes and challenge your audience to implement them.

And then conclude with poignant stories and powerful images of the struggles of specific people, putting a human face on the issue being discussed. This makes it easier for your audience to say "Yes" to your pitch.

Listen to speeches and comments by politicians, religious leaders, teachers, social activists, and others. They do this all the time in an effort to inspire and mobilize their audiences.

One of the best speakers I've heard was a college professor speaking on Latin American politics. His argument was impassioned, organized, and well-researched. His presentation and his speaking style had such an impact on me that I still have it in mind thirty years later.

You know you've made an impact when audience members say things like: "I never thought of it that way." "You've inspired me to try the things I've always been afraid of." "Your presentation changed my life."

You've inspired them to act.

TAKEAWAY: Inspiring others to act is one of the most powerful and noble accomplishments – be sure to include it in your presentation whenever appropriate.

Lesson 48
Send Thank-you Notes

I can no other answer make, but, thanks, and thanks.

~ William Shakespeare

*Make it a habit to tell people thank you. To express
your appreciation, sincerely and without the
expectation of anything in return.
Truly appreciate those around you, and you'll soon
find many others around you.*

~ Ralph Marston

If you were lucky enough to have parents who insisted that you write thank-you notes whenever you slept over or ate dinner at a friend's house, this lesson will be second nature to you.

Unfortunately, at a young age it's not easy to appreciate how valuable that habit will become later in life.

In these times of email, texting, Facebook, and Twitter, the handwritten thank-you note is a rarity indeed. But don't discount it. It is one of the many tools in your toolkit that will help distinguish you from other speakers.

If you aren't in the habit now of sending thank-you notes to the people who invited you to speak, you should get started.

Why should you write thank-you notes after a presentation?

It's the right thing to do.

Sending a thank-you note is polite and signals to the recipient that you are grateful for the opportunity to speak. This may help create future opportunities to speak again.

Generally speaking, people like to receive mail and be acknowledged. Receiving a thank-you note, especially one that is unexpected, makes the recipient feel good.

Who among us does not like to receive a thank-you note?

A thank-you note helps the recipient remember you.

So few people send thank-you notes that you have increased the chances of being remembered by adding a personal touch to your relationship with the program organizers.

Thank-you notes are quick, easy, and relatively inexpensive. They demonstrate to the recipient that you are organized, thoughtful, and value the experience.

I prefer to send thank-you notes handwritten on custom-made, hand-stitched cards with fabric backing crafted by *Sweet Jane Paperie* (www.sweetjanepaperie.com), a company owned by my sister. They are unique, tasteful, and show the recipient that I'm organized, thoughtful, and, most of all, that I value our relationship.

And be sure to send the note regardless of whether you were compensated in any way for your presentation.

TAKEAWAY: Thank-you notes, especially handwritten ones, will help to distinguish you from most other speakers.

Part 4

Into the Arena:
Setting Out on Your Journey

Create Your Own Opportunities

We are all faced with a series of great opportunities
brilliantly disguised as impossible situations.

~ Charles R. Swindoll

Don't wait for extraordinary opportunities.
Seize common occasions and make them great.
Weak people wait for opportunities;
strong people make them.

~ Orison Swett Marden

All too often, we wait until we're forced into action before doing anything.

With public speaking, we go kicking and screaming to the front of the class to give a presentation. We anticipate briefings at work with about as much relish as a root canal. The experience is filled with angst and punctuated by relief that we even made it through alive.

But now that you have your road map, you know it doesn't have to be that way.

Like everything else, the best way to improve your public speaking is to get out there and do it. Finding your local Toastmasters group is a great way to get practice.

Beyond Toastmasters, you may be at a loss about what to speak on and where to speak. Don't worry, that's the easy part.

Many of us get conditioned to hate public speaking because we're usually forced to do it, on a topic we don't care about, in front of our peers, and at a time in our life when we're scared how the audience will react.

If you're creating your own opportunities, you can choose your own topic and your own audience.

Think about what you know, what you're passionate about, what you're curious about, and what experiences you've had in your life. Any and all of this is material for your presentations.

It could be about an amazing vacation you took or how to cook. It could be how to care for pets or how to fly a plane. It could be anything under the sun that you are qualified to speak about.

You may wonder, "Who cares what I have to say?"

Elementary, high school, and college students care. Retired people, church congregations, and staff at local companies care. Boy Scouts, Girl Scouts, and any other kind of scouts you can imagine care. Your local Rotary Club, Lions Club, Kiwanis Club, and Chambers of Commerce care.

Remember, you're creating your own opportunities because you know that public speaking is a keystone habit. Imagine all of the new people you'll meet and opportunities you'll create for yourself by offering to speak to groups.

TAKEAWAY: Creating your own opportunities to speak will not only improve your speaking, it will also change your life.

Get in the Arena

Our deepest fear is not that we are inadequate.
Our deepest fear is that we are powerful
beyond measure. It is our light, not our darkness that
most frightens us. We ask ourselves, Who am I to be
brilliant, gorgeous, talented, fabulous? Actually,
who are you not to be? You are a child of God.
Your playing small does not serve the world. There
is nothing enlightened about shrinking so that other
people won't feel insecure around you. We are all
meant to shine, as children do. We were born to make
manifest the glory of God that is within us. It's not just in
some of us; it's in everyone. And as we let our own
light shine, we unconsciously give other people
permission to do the same. As we are liberated from our
own fear, our presence automatically liberates others.

~ Marianne Williamson

At the beginning of this journey, I wrote about beliefs, the importance of deciding and committing, and the need to get out there and do it.

I never thought I could be a public speaker. My fears had gotten deep inside me. I was paralyzed.

Over time, I learned two important things: the mechanics of public speaking and the nature of fear.

Here are some of my most important takeaways for you to put in your toolbox for your journey:

- Public speaking is always about serving the audience. It's about suppressing the ego and expanding the heart.

- You can't think yourself into being a public speaker. You can't read your way into being a public speaker. Although thinking and reading are important, you actually have to do it.

- It is in the doing that we learn to manage our fear. Take that first step and get in the arena.

- It's simple but it's not easy. Nothing of real value is handed to us. We will have to work hard and make glorious, empowering mistakes. Mistakes are the trumpets that declare our determination to outwit fear.

- When you get confused and are unsure of the path ahead, fear not. That is not you failing; it's you finding your way. It's you getting out of your comfort zone. And that's where mistakes – and progress – are made.

- Become a Chinese farmer who knows that there is no "good" and "bad." It is what it is.

Fear is a familiar, snuggly blanket we think keeps us warm and protected from what we don't want to do.

Fear is the constant activity we use to kid ourselves that we don't *really* want something when, in fact, we do.

Fear urges us to procrastinate, convincing us we will never be good enough.

Fear whispers in our ear that we have to be perfect.

That warm, protective blanket is actually choking us. It distorts our vision of the past and robs us of what's possible for the future.

Give yourself a rest from fear, and step into the arena. I know you're going to do great. Good luck!

TAKEAWAY: Don't let fear stop you from changing your life for the better. Speak from the heart, with sincerity and authenticity, for the benefit of the audience.

The Takeaways

Lesson 1   A good road map will help you manage your fear.

Lesson 2   Everything you need is already within you. It's time to believe in yourself.

Lesson 3   The key to your success is hard work focused on a specific objective.

Lesson 4   Managing fear can provide the key to unlocking all of your dreams.

Lesson 5   Contemplate the questions that need to be answered in order to reach your destination.

Lesson 6   Keep limiting self-judgment to a minimum.

Lesson 7   Remember, plateaus are a critical part of mastering your subject matter.

Lesson 8   Let go of "perfect" and serve your audience.

Lesson 9   Develop a plan today of the next steps you will take to manage your procrastination.

Lesson 10   Get off your "buts" and take control of your own destiny.

Lesson 11   Paying close attention to critiques of your performance will get you further than blame and procrastination.

Lesson 12   Develop public speaking as a keystone habit that will change your life.

Lesson 13   Effective public speaking is a conversation focused on the needs of the audience, not your ego.

Lesson 14   Put the needs of your audience first in the course of your conversation.

Lesson 15	Keeping the audience as your top priority helps reduce fear and improve performance.
Lesson 16	Success or failure happens long before you get on stage. Thorough preparation can turn you into a winner every time.
Lesson 17	Knowing the audience is important in creating a connection and distinguishing yourself from other speakers.
Lesson 18	Serve your audience by delivering a well-structured, logical presentation in an authentic way.
Lesson 19	Put a system of collecting, processing, and organizing information in place for ease in developing your presentation.
Lesson 20	Determine your theme and major points, personalize your presentation when possible, and re-work your draft.
Lesson 21	Be conscious of the flow of your presentation. Start out strong, follow your established arc, and close by inspiring your audience.
Lesson 22	Public speaking is about the audience, not the PowerPoint presentation. The fewer the words, the more powerful your message. Think about not using PowerPoint at all!
Lesson 23	Provide handout material that contains important information and is impactful.
Lesson 24	Dress one notch above the audience without being distracting.
Lesson 25	Record your presentations as the best way to improve your public speaking as quickly as possible.
Lesson 26	Get comfortable with the meeting room so you're ready to focus on delivering a great presentation.
Lesson 27	Develop rituals for turbocharging your passion before a presentation.
Lesson 28	Let your voice and body language work with you to show that you're comfortable in front of the group.

Lesson 29	Write your own introduction highlighting the most important information that the audience should hear.
Lesson 30	Grab the audience from the very first sentence and give them a reason to go on a journey with you.
Lesson 31	Building a connection is about engaging the audience as quickly and genuinely as possible through the use of props, body language, and expressions of your personality.
Lesson 32	Strengthen the connection between you and your audience by sharing something about yourself when appropriate.
Lesson 33	Use appropriate props to increase audience attention and to get your message across more effectively.
Lesson 34	Engaging, impactful, inspirational material for your presentations is all around you. Stretch your imagination to find something that will connect with the audience.
Lesson 35	Don't stray from the main theme of your presentation or you risk confusing your audience.
Lesson 36	Eliminating verbal fillers will help the audience stay engaged and make you look better prepared.
Lesson 37	Think about other forms of human than telling a joke if you are not a seasoned joke-teller.
Lesson 38	Know the dynamics of the room and your audience and so your best to influence them in a positive way, minimizing distractions.
Lesson 39	Only use a lectern if absolutely necessary and practice using it effectively.
Lesson 40	Use preparation time to become familiar with the microphone. It can make or break your presentation.
Lesson 41	Never apologize in the opening of your presentation.
Lesson 42	Your job is to be sincere, authentic, passionate, and inspiring. Your eyes will show all of that and more.

Lesson 43   Practice building pauses into your presentation to make powerful points.

Lesson 44   Embrace mistakes as necessary bridges to success.

Lesson 45   Never lose your temper or your sense of humor when something goes wrong.

Lesson 46   Entertain questions as appropriate, but don't get sidetracked. Never close your presentation with a question-and-answer segment.

Lesson 47   Inspiring others to act is one of the most powerful and noble accomplishments – be sure to include it in your presentation whenever appropriate.

Lesson 48   Thank-you notes, especially handwritten ones, will help to distinguish you from most other speakers.

Lesson 49   Creating your own opportunities to speak will not only improve your speaking, it will also change your life.

Lesson 50   Don't let fear stop you from changing your life for the better. Speak from the heart, with sincerity and authenticity, for the benefit of the audience.

Acknowledgements

Two people were instrumental in pushing me to become a public speaker:

Dick Ward, then Vice Chancellor of the University of Illinois at Chicago with whom I worked in the late 1980s and early 90s, required that I tackle my fear and start speaking.

Doug Dretke at the Correctional Management Institute of Texas (CMIT) provided the environment for further development of my public speaking skills for the six years I worked there.

Thanks to Jim Randel (www.theskinnyon.com) for his enthusiasm and support in this project.

Special thanks to my wife, Jennifer, for the meticulous editing she gave the manuscript. She took on the project as if it were her own and raised the quality of the final product several degrees.

Thanks to my parents, Jane Serio and the late Dr. Joseph Serio, for encouraging me to see the connections among things and people, for encouraging me to create something special for my audiences, and for encouraging me not to follow the crowd too closely. It has made all the difference in my speaking style.

Finally, thanks to all who read the manuscript and offered feedback: Brent Boepple, Carrie Carroll, Jim Comer, Jim Dodson, John Graham, Cherrie Greco, Mary Hayden, Roxane Marek, Michael Mugno, Jim Napolitano, Will Oliver, Stephen Plezia, Kim Schnurbush, Frank Serio, Grace Serio, John Serio, Paul Sheldon, and Carolyn Torella.

Thanks to you for reading this book. Now it's your turn to get out and speak. It will change your life.

Our special gift to you:

A FREE copy of our article,
"The #1 Reason You Don't Get What You Want"

Are you ready to have clarity around why you're struggling so you can start to make progress toward your goals?

This article will show you:

- The five myths about what's holding you back
- How these myths work against you
- Three powerful tools to make significant progress
- How your life will change once you master these tools

Stop waiting for something to change when you keep doing the same thing. Download this FREE ARTICLE and learn what you can do to have the life you want.

DOWNLOAD NOW at:

www.joeserio.com

Also in the *Get the Nerve™ Series*

Overcoming Fear:
50 Lessons on Being Bold and Living the Dream

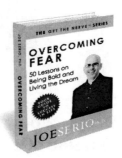

Take a good look at your life—is there something you would change, if you could? Why is it that you don't already have whatever it is you're longing for?

- A successful career you enjoy
- Loving, peaceful relationships
- The time and money to do what you want

Whether you know it or not, chances are fear has become an obstacle in your path to reaching your goals. Until you learn how to move past it, you'll continue to be stuck.

Stop fear in its tracks, and Get the Nerve™ to have the career, relationships, and lifestyle you want!

ORDER NOW!

www.joeserio.com

Also in the *Get the Nerve*™ *Series*

The **Get the Nerve Mastery Program**™!

How would your life be different if you could have:

- Greater confidence
- More quality time with your loved ones
- Increased flexibility
- Happier relationships
- The ability to say, "I can!"

Part of the *Get the Nerve*™ *Series*, this six-DVD set brings you six hours of success training direct from Dr. Joe himself, including how to overcome fear, eliminate procrastination, create healthy relationships at work and home, be an effective role model, confidently give presentations, and more.

Though these DVDs are complete with presentations, you can pop one into the CD player in your car to listen while you drive.

Want to feel like you can conquer the world?

ORDER NOW at:

www.joeserio.com

Book Dr. Joe for your next training or event!

Dr. Joe is an expert in organizational behavior and can inspire your audience to see new possibilities and potential. He uses music and his own incredible life experiences to entertain and connect with your audience, enabling them to make unique connections between work and home so they can create improvements in *all* areas.

His most popular keynotes and trainings include:

- Overcoming Fear
- Time Management and Organizational Skills
- Effective Communication
- Leadership and Legacy

To book Dr. Joe for your event, please visit:

www.joeserio.com

Or email us at:

drjoe@joeserio.com

Biography

Dr. Joe Serio used to be afraid of everything. Then he did some crazy stuff, like move to Moscow to investigate the Russian Mafia, and now he's not scared of anything (except his wife). Through all his incredible experiences – rescuing people from mobsters, traveling the world, getting a Ph.D., learning to play music in front of huge audiences, and surviving his childhood as one of twelve kids – he became an expert on how to Get the Nerve™ to do anything. Dr. Joe teaches his philosophy to thousands of people in his teleseminars, trainings, workshops, and events.

Follow him on…

Facebook: facebook.com/JoeSerioEnterprises

Twitter: twitter.com/JoeSerioSpeaks

YouTube: youtube.com/JoeSerioEnterprises

LinkedIn: linkedin.com/JoeSerioEnterprises

CPSIA information can be obtained at www.ICGtesting.com
Printed in the USA
LVOW12s1918261213

366976LV00003B/5/P